Astrology, Psychology, and The Four Elements

*An Energy Approach to Astrology &
Its Use in the Counseling Arts*

Stephen Arroyo

(Author of *Astrology, Karma & Transformation*)

CRCS PUBLICATIONS
Post Office Box 1460
Sebastopol, California 95472
U.S.A.

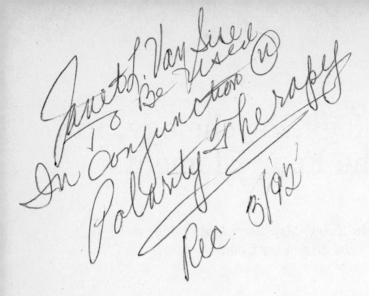

Janet L. Van Sice
To Be Used
In Conjunction ©
Polarity Therapy
Rec. 3/93

© 1975 by Stephen Arroyo

INTERNATIONAL STANDARD BOOK NUMBERS:
0-916360-01-6 (paperback)
0-916360-02-4 (hardcover)
LIBRARY OF CONGRESS CATALOG CARD NUMBER: 75-27828
Published simultaneously in the United States and Canada by:
CRCS Publications
Distributed in the United States by CRCS Publications
Distributed in England by L. N. Fowler & Co. Ltd.

Designed by Kathleen Mullins
See acknowledgements for other copyright information.

Cover Design: Collage by Betty Spry (original approx. 39 inches square), based on a Mandala from *Secret of the Golden Flower*, translated and explained by Richard Wilhelm, reproduced by permission of Harcourt Brace Jovanovich, Inc.

STEPHEN ARROYO holds an MA degree in psychology and the California State License in Marriage and Family Counseling and has maintained a busy astrological counseling practice since 1970. Experienced in many methods of psychotherapy, healing, yoga, and other transformative techniques, he has taught astrology, Polarity Therapy, and other healing arts at various schools and centers on the West Coast, including regular classes at JFK University and Sacramento City College. He has contributed dozens of articles to astrological magazines and journals, and his MA thesis synthesizing astrology and psychology (incorporated in this book) was awarded the Astrology Prize by the British Astrological Association. He is also the author of the highly original book *Astrology, Karma & Transformation: The Inner Dimensions of the Birth Chart.*

Other Books by The Author

Astrology, Karma & Transformation: The Inner Dimensions of the Birth Chart

Relationships & Life Cycles: Modern Dimensions of Astrology

The Practice & Profession of Astrology: Rebuilding Our Lost Connections With The Cosmos

The Jupiter/Saturn Conference Lectures: Explorations in Modern Astrology (Co-authored with Liz Greene)

Acknowledgements

Some of the material incorporated in this book has been printed in the form of articles in Dell's HOROSCOPE magazine, Popular Library's astrology magazines (such as ZODIAC and AQUARIAN ASTROLOGY), and Llewellyn's ASTROLOGY NOW newspaper. We appreciate, therefore, the editors' permission to bring it forth in this entirely revised and enlarged presentation.

I would like to express special gratitude to Pauline Hutson, April Fletcher, and Barbara McEnerney for their typing, proofreading, and constructive suggestions. If any errors remain in the book, they can be attributed to the author's negligence.

I am also indebted to Betty Spry for allowing the use of her beautiful collage on the cover of the book, to Pacia Ryneal for her artistic talents, and to Kathleen Arroyo for endless help and patience in her design and layout of the book.

I wish to express my thanks also to Jim Feil, Dr. Pierre Pannetier, and Dr. Randolph Stone for helping me to gain some degree of insight into the workings of the four elements, and also to the many friends and students who have encouraged my writing and teaching.

Finally, we appreciate the permission of the following publishers to make use of copyrighted material from their books:

From ACCENT ON FORM by L.L. Whyte. Copyright 1954 by Lancelot Law White. Used with permission of Harper & Row, Publishers, Inc.

From PSYCHIC DISCOVERIES BEHIND THE IRON CURTAIN by Ostrander & Schroeder. Copyright 1970 by Sheila Ostrander & Lynn Schroeder. Used with permission of Prentice-Hall, Inc., Englewood Cliffs, N.J.

From ASTROLOGICAL BIRTH CONTROL by Ostrander & Schroeder. Copyright 1972 by Sheila Ostrander & Lynn Schroeder. Used with permission of Prentice-Hall, Inc.

From BORN TO HEAL by Ruth Montgomery. Copyright 1973 by Ruth Montgomery & Dena L. Smith, M.D. Used with permission of Coward, McCann & Geoghegan, Inc.

From THE COLLECTED WORKS OF C.G. JUNG, ed. by Gerhard Adler, Michael Fordham, Herbert Read, and William McGuire, trans. by R.F.C. Hull, Bollingen Series XX, vol. 9i, The Archetypes and the Collective Unconscious. Copyright 1959 & 1969 by Bollingen Foundation. Reprinted by permission of Princeton University Press.

From THE UNDISCOVERED SELF by C.G. Jung. Mentor Books, NY, 1958. Used with permission of Little, Brown and Company.

To Dane Rudhyar,
In appreciation for his encouragement,
inspiration, and uncompromising purity of vision.

Astrology is assured recognition from psychology, without further restriction, because astrology represents the summation of all psychological knowledge of antiquity.

— C.G. Jung, Commentary on *The Secret of the Golden Flower*

The task of science is not merely to identify the changing structural pattern in everything, but *to see it as simple*. Science starts with the assumption which is always present, though it may be unconscious, may be forgotten, or may sometimes even be denied: *There exists a simple order in nature; a simple way of representing experience is possible; the task of science is to discover it.*

— L.L. Whyte, *Accent on Form*

Contents

Prologue

A new kind of astrology is being born at this time. It is still rather unformed, not totally coordinated, not fully adapted to social needs, and in need of a great deal of encouragement and support from its parents. Just as a baby falls many times in learning to walk, this new kind of astrology is having its ups and downs, and it occasionally falls flat on its face. Like all children, this growing entity requires concentrated attention from its parents in order to develop its potentialities to the full. And, although a parent cannot sit back with satisfaction to contemplate a job well done until the child is fully healthy and self-sufficient, the very process of encouraging the growth and development of the child is incentive enough to continue the work. This new kind of astrology takes traditional theories and attitudes and turns them inside out, exposing at times a degenerated mass of contradictions and empty banalities, and at other times an inspiring essence of universal truth. The new kind of astrologer, therefore, roots out the imperfections and attempts to penetrate to a level of understanding that will illuminate an entirely new approach not only to astrology but also to man himself.

The breakthroughs in the field of psychology made in the first half of this century are only now beginning to be assimilated into the mass consciousness, although they began to influence astrology as early as the 1930's. It is only recently however that the process of assimilation has gained sufficient momentum that a great number of astrologers and astrology students are feeling the need to re-structure and re-define astrological traditions and the purpose of astrology itself. This restructuring process began with Dane Rudhyar's *The Astrology of Personality* in 1936, and since then it has slowly gained speed and popularity. The development of this new kind of astrology has been so slow mainly because it takes many years for the mass consciousness to change and for astrologers to outgrow the old structure that they learned when first studying astrology. But the consciousness of the times has changed, and astrologers are slowly realizing that most methods of interpretation and practice that were appropriate for people in the 1920's are irrelevant to people living and growing today.

The specific ways in which this new astrology differs from the older methods are explained in this book in great detail, but I would like to emphasize one point. In most traditional forms of astrological practice, wherein the astrologer was essentially serving as a fortune-teller, it was assumed that the birth-chart revealed the circumstances that one would encounter in life and that these circumstances *in the outer world* were predictable and for the most part unalterable. However, it is obvious that the predictability of anything varies according to its level of complexity. For example, a simple animal cell or chemical compound is usually predictable since its nature is simple, since there few variables, and since it has no consciousness or capacity for alternative ways of reacting. The weather is less predictable primarily because there are many unknown variables, although it may still be predicted in many cases based on an understanding of known variables. A human being is least predictable because he has some degree of reason, will, and detachment, and because he is therefore capable of unlimited variable responses. And, as he gains more consciousness, he is even less predictable than before. Hence, a highly conscious person may need only an intimation of a possible event or experience in order to learn a certain lesson or to gain a particular insight, whereas one who is less conscious may need to experience a more definite and concrete outer circumstance in order to gain the same understanding. It seems to me that an individual is predictable precisely in proportion to his lack of conscious awareness. Hence, the new type of astrology to which I am referring is primarily oriented toward those who have taken some definite steps to gain increased self-knowledge.

It is true that one is born with a certain birth-chart, with a certain pattern of "karma" or emotional-mental-physical tendencies. However, the circumstances that one will confront are to a large extent programmed by what one expresses. In other words, you get back what you put out; everything returns to its source. If one expresses impatience and self-righteousness, for example, he or she will automatically *elicit* such responses from others. It is useless to blame one's birth-chart for one's self-created misery. The emphasis in a modern, constructive use of astrology should be working with, modifying, or transmuting the natal energy attunement in order that the most positive expression of the energies can be manifested. I have tried therefore in this book to emphasize a deeper *understanding* of basic astrological factors and a deeper appreciation of the purpose of all astrological techniques.

This book is written in two distinct parts. The first six chapters of Part I were originally included in a master's thesis for an M.A. degree in psychology at California State University, Sacramento. The original thesis, before extensive editing, was awarded the 1973 Astrology Prize by the British Astrological Association as the most valuable contribution to astrology during that year. My main orientation in writing that section was to clarify various approaches to astrology and to reveal its practical utility, especially in ways directly related to the field of psychology. Although it was written primarily for those who are totally unfamiliar with the astrological point of view, students or practitioners of astrology can also benefit from it. For, not only does it contribute to a synthesis and deeper understanding of astrological premises, but it is also useful as an aid to answering the endless questions of the thoughtful general public or the prejudicial criticisms of the uninformed.

Part II of the book provides a foundation for all astrological theory in terms of energy, through a systematic explanation of the ancient concept of the four elements. Since the elements describe the actual energies symbolized by astrological factors, an understanding of their principles enables one to synthesize the meaning of a birth-chart in a practical and immediate way. It seems to me that the biggest obstacle in a student's learning astrology or in a practitioner's ability to use astrology in a practical, helpful way is the lack of synthesizing methods presented in astrological writings. There are so many beginning textbooks available nowadays, but only rarely does one find in print an explanation of how to penetrate to the core meaning of astrological factors or of how to see a simple pattern of order within the endless combinations represented in birth-charts. It should also be emphasized here that, since Part II deals mainly with the *basic principles* of the elements, it was necessary in many cases to generalize in order to bring out the essential principle being discussed. Readers should, however, be cautioned not to identify with only the Sun sign element (or indeed with any other *one* factor) in their charts as they procede through this volume. As I have tried to clarify in the book, each chart factor is an independent emphasis within the pattern of the whole, but a strong factor does not dominate the entire pattern to the *exclusion* of other points of emphasis. It should also be stated that, although the term "energy" may seem rather nebulous to some readers, our language simply does not provide more precise words. After all, light energy, if considered as an octave, is only one of about seventy-five octaves in the frequency ranges of the *recognized* electromagnetic spectrum. Attempting to describe transcendent energies with our limited language has been a difficult and challenging task, and I hope the reader will excuse any failure to communicate the rather subtle meanings involved.

The approach that one assumes in studying any phenomenon is naturally based upon the purpose one has in mind, whether consciously or unconsciously. In other words, what one wants to *do* with one's conclusions determines the approach taken. In this book, my purpose is to provide a background and a framework for understanding astrology in modern terms and to elucidate both the structure and the application of this science in relation to contemporary psychology, psychotherapy, and energy concepts. Hence, for the most part, I have omitted references to more "occult" or "esoteric"aspects of astrology, not because I believe that such an approach is without value, but merely because it is beyond the scope of this work.

In order that new ideas can prosper, we have to be free of "known" presuppositions so that a sense of wonder can illuminate our perception. Such freedom and openness is always a characteristic of true science. Clearing the ground of intellectual and emotional prejudices is necessary in order to achieve this freedom, and it is for this reason that I have herein devoted so many pages to a systematic critique of current "scientific" and, psychological methods. Today, many people are seeking a more unified and comprehensive view of life than is available in the over-specialized disciplines commonly taught in traditional colleges and universities. There is a growing demand for a whole and satisfying participation with the cycles of life, and astrology can provide just that. As the physicist-philosopher L.L. Whyte has written, "The deepest aesthetic and scientific principle lies in a tendency toward simplicty, order, elegance, form." Astrology reveals the overall pattern of simplicity, order, elegance, and form that operates throughout the universe and, in particular, within every individual.

Within the field of psychology, there are dozens of "theories of personality" which attempt to discover and define some semblance of order within the character and life-style of the individual. Every theory of personality assumes that there is such a thing as "human nature" which the new-born brings with him into this world, chiefly in the form of general predispositions and potentialities rather than specific traits. The problem with all the personality theories commonly utilized in psychology today is that each is inherently biased toward the sort of person who shares certain characteristics with the inventor of the theory. In other words, since the theoretician assumes that everybody is really like himself down deep, and since he has no cosmic framework to enable him to gain a broader perspective on humankind, the use of such limited and biased theories in actual practice has profoundly destructive effects. If however, as the evidence in this book indicates, astrology is indeed a language that describes the very energies that activate a human being, it could very well be the most accurate way we have of describing what is truly the "human nature" of each individual. After utilizing astrology extensively for the past nine years, this is certainly how it seems to me; and, over the past few years in my practice, I have gradually let all the other theories go by the wayside. To me, astrology is without a doubt the most accurate and comprehensive means of understanding human personality, behavior, change, and growth.

I have often been asked why astrology has witnessed such renewed popularity in recent years. I think part of the answer lies in the fact that Western culture no longer has any viable mythology to sustain it. Myth always serves as a vitalizing force in any culture by showing man's relationship to a larger, more universal reality. People have always needed a pattern of order to guide their collective lives and to infuse their individual experience with meaning.* In this sense, astrology comprises within itself an

---

*Cf. *Beyond Stonehenge* by Gerald Hawkins; pub. by Harper & Row, 1973. The author is a Boston University astronomer who has found a "cosmic orientation" in nearly every great civilization throughout history.

entire mythological framework. Professor Joseph Campbell writes that "Man cannot maintain himself in the universe without belief in some arrangement of the general inheritance of myth. In fact, the fullness of his life would even seem to stand in direct ratio to the depth and range not of his rational thought, but of his local mythology." Campbell states that there are three essential functions of myth: "to elicit a sense of awe," "to render a cosmology," and "to initiate the individual into the realities of his own psyche." As so many people are discovering today, the proper use of astrology fulfills all these three functions. Hence, if we agree with Campbell's definition of myth, I think we must agree that astrology, as it has for ages past, provides a vital and practical mythology for our times.

Part I

Astrology & Psychology

1

Modern Science & Psychology Today

The human phenomenon must be measured on a cosmic scale.
— Teilhard de Chardin

Just as we are now undergoing a world-wide revolution in communications, social forms, and international relations, so we are also in the midst of a revolution in our views of man and the universe. The revolving wheel of change never ceases, but nowadays we seem to be at the crucial point at which an old cycle of life is ending and the initial characteristics of the coming cycle are beginning to become apparent. Science as a whole and psychology as an independent discipline must respond to these changes (and to the changing needs of modern men and women) in creative and open-minded ways. Most people today still look toward "science" and to so-called "experts" for answers to our modern dilemma; but all too often psychologists, psychiatrists, and other specialists who purport to *know* the answers really have little to offer the common man. The meaning and significance of personal experience (the true domain of any person-centered psychological inquiry) is only rarely illuminated by these specialists. A few specialists *have* taken significant steps toward a synthesis of modern knowledge in a way man's deepest being can respond to, for example Dr. Carl G. Jung and Père Teilhard de Chardin. But for the most part, even those who pay lip service to the high ideals of searching for truth, unifying our modern world-view, and helping our fellow man all too often refuse to take risks, preferring to remain cloistered in their professional specialties. It is only rarely that a man of great creativity and courage, willing to bear the critical abuse of his contemporaries and colleagues, takes it upon himself to act on these high ideals.

In Western culture today, we find that man is increasingly alienated from himself and his culture. He is out of touch with his fundamental human roots. His traditions and cultural values are breaking down or being discarded. Man today badly needs to re-establish contact with the essence of the human tradition and the core of his psychic life, both of which transcend place and time. So far as I know, no one theory of "personality" within the domain of psychology has achieved an understanding and description of Universal Man. Therefore, it is time to look elsewhere, toward theories and ideas and experiences that are true for every human being. This is of course a large order; but a global society is emerging, and we had better pave the way for its peaceful birth by gaining an understanding of what man really is. What is the nature of this new world order on the horizon? Huston Smith (1971), Professor of Philosophy at MIT and author of *The Religions of Man,* states:

> There are . . . three great civilizations: Western, East Asian (Chinese), and South Asian (Indian). Historically, in their main periods, each of these specialized in one of these three problem areas: the West on nature, China on social relations, and India on psychological relations. If the above hypothesis is true, each civilization stands to learn from the other two in the areas it has neglected.

> We can take from China respect for family, attitude toward age, and attitude toward the personal sphere as opposed to the empire, i.e., a higher loyalty to the community centered in the home. From India, as Gordon Allport has observed, of the four goals of man which India recognizes, i.e., pleasure, worldly success, duty, and liberation, the West has been concerned almost entirely with the first two, with slight attention to duty and no attention to liberation. There is also the noting of distinctive human types, which, although abused in the Indian caste system, is nevertheless a valid insight . . . .

> Second, the new civilization will be more ecological. As noted earlier, the West has been preoccupied with nature. China and India have also been concerned with nature, but in the spirit of Wordsworth rather than Galileo. The Western sense is one of dominance over nature . . . Presently there is a groping for originality, but what about quality? . . . I believe that we will come back to the glories of simplicity in the ecological aspect of the new civilization.

> My third prediction about the new civilization is that when the time comes there will be a more spiritual orientation toward the

world. Whereas in the 19th century we view nature as a machine, now in the 20th century we are viewing nature as an organism, with less determinism and more freedom. Can we extrapolate from mechanical in the 17th to 19th, biological in the 20th, to psychological in the 21st century?

Finally, we will be entering into the new world civilization to the extent that we are able to achieve a new pattern of life that is some kind of synthesis of these three emphases from past civilizations — nature, fellow man, and self. (p. 1 ff.)

Hans Stossel (1959) expresses man's modern need in this way:

It is essential today to come to a deeper, spiritual, cosmic understanding, and that this alone is the necessity of our age and the need of this century should be revelation. This should be a time when man stands with a greater knowledge (not only a belief) of how to be at one with the universe.

It is this synthesis, this union of man with the natural world, and this feeling of oneness with the universe that astrology can contribute to modern man's welfare. As psychologist Robert L. Marrone (1971) writes, "Man's thoughts on nature and his relation to nature have, over recorded history, diminished him or enlarged him, separated him from the natural world or fused him with a cyclic universe." Modern man's feeling of separation from the natural world and lack of identity with the cosmos explains why (since this is the cultural *zeitgeist* now) astrology has to be "proven" before many people will accept it as a valid science or art. Almost every culture that we know of had some form of astrology; and this is not attributable to their lack of modern "enlightenment," but rather to their immediate sense of unity with the cosmic environment. More than anything else, the popular pseudo-scientific prejudices and adherence to out-dated scientific theories among working scientists, educators, and the general public stand in the way of a new synthesis of knowledge and a new hope for man's future. It seems that most academic psychologists, in particular, are doing exactly what Robert Oppenheimer (1971) warned against: i.e., striving to mold a science of psychology on a physics that is already outmoded. If we look at modern physics, we see incredible diversity and such notions as anti-matter and indeterminancy, the descriptions of which sound more like a mystic's account of religious ecstasy than what we are accustomed to expect from a scientific treatise. And yet, researchers in psychology, with a few notable exceptions, continue to operate as if they were bio-chemists or reflex physicists. Therefore, although astrological practitioners can indeed benefit from an acquaintance with certain insights and procedures of modern psychology, they should be cautious about underestimating astrology itself and overestimating the efficacy of present-day psychology in their efforts to achieve a more sophisticated and respectable type of astrological practice. As C.G. Jung stated, "Obviously astrology offers much to psychology, but that which the latter can contribute to its elder sister is less obvious."

Science is a powerful tool, as is astrology. The knowledge we gain through these methods can be used in two ways: manipulation or appreciation. Unfortunately, science in the West has so far been used primarily for the former, not only in the physical sciences, but also in psychology. As the physicist-philosopher L.L. Whyte (1954) writes, "Science itself could benefit from a fuller recognition of the unconscious preferences which have guided its historical development and still persist today." It is time that science as a whole, and astrology and psychology in particular, make a new commitment to the search for truth and understanding rather than just collecting isolated facts. Although astrology also has been and can be used for manipulative purposes, its synthesis with the better insights of psychology can provide us with a penetrating means of more deeply appreciating ourselves, our universe, and other human beings.

While some scientists (psychologists included) blandly voice the idea that new and creative approaches are necessary in order that science can progress, they, by the very nature of their attitudes and personal identification with "science," prevent the development of such approaches. In other words, they have no understanding of the truly *creative* process (as differentiated from the mere assemblage and correlation of facts). Many do not realize that the split in their own personalities (professionally "objective" while personally and privately "subjective") prevents the creative act from occurring within them. This is so because creativity is an outgrowth of individual human wholeness and integration, or of the striving toward such wholeness. As Rudin (1968) writes in his book *Psychotherapy and Religion*, "One cannot escape from his own soul without mutilating his life and also condemning himself to illness in the physical realm and to a perfidious, stereotyped productivity in the intellectual" (pp. 29-30). It appears that the followers and disciples of the true pioneers in any field, assured that they have found the truth, soon become rigid and fanatical, freezing the ideas of the original theoretician. This has the effect of stifling new developments for decades. This same process has also occurred in some astrological circles, resulting in further fragmentation and discord in a field that desperately needs open-minded unity.

Those who make the creative breakthroughs, those whose names are revered in succeeding generations, are always those who are truly open to the new. This very openness naturally takes the creative person into areas of thought and research that are professionally unorthodox and culturally unconventional. As Alfred North Whitehead observed, almost all really new ideas have a certain aspect of foolishness when they are first produced. We have only to look at the names and lives of some of the greatest creators in Western culture to realize how many of them were occupied with areas of study that were officially taboo at the time. Einstein (1954) talked about the "mystical" experience of original insight and the "religious" feeling of true understanding:

> The most beautiful and most profound emotion we can experi-
> ence is the sensation of the mystical. It is the power of all true
> science. To know that what is impenetrable to us really exists,
> manifesting itself as the highest wisdom and the most radiant
> beauty which our dull faculties can comprehend only in their
> most primitive forms — this knowledge, this feeling, is at the
> center of true religiousness.

C.G. Jung not only used astrology as a psychological tool in his practice, but also spent years doing research into the psychological aspects of alchemical symbolism. Sigmund Freud (1970) wrote in a letter toward the end of his career, "If I had my life to live over again I should devote myself to psychic research rather than psychoanalysis." The astronomer and physicist Kepler (1967) tells us that he had a strong desire *not* to believe in astrology's efficacy, but that "the unfailing concurrence of stellar configurations and sublunary events compelled my unwilling belief." Other well-known astrologer-scientists are Francis Bacon, Benjamin Franklin, Lord Napier (inventor of logarithms), and Isaac Newton. In fact it was Newton who, when asked what he wanted to study at Cambridge, reportedly replied: "Mathematics, so that I may test astrology." Furthermore, Newton, when chided by Haley (the discoverer of the comet) for believing such a superstition, is reported to have said: "It is evident that you have not looked into astrology; I have."

The more we discover about life, the more we tend to arrive at ideas which unify many areas of life and many intellectual disciplines. Such unifying ideas are desperately needed today, especially in the field of psychology, the science that deals most intimately with people's lives. It is evident to me that astrology is just that pattern of order and unity that psychology today is lacking. The unity, health, and integration of the individual man is the starting point for the health and viability of his society. How can a society whose educational institutions preach a fragmented approach to life and a distorted view of the world produce a healthy creative individual? What is presently needed most of all, particularly in the educational establishment, is a thorough questioning of our assumptions about the nature of man and the meaning of existence. If we are honest with ourselves, then we can be open to what *is*. Then, in order to establish a type of psychology (and astrology) focusing on individual health and fulfillment, we can begin to develop a true science of life, dealing with the entire psycho-physical being, the focal point of which is consciousness itself. But before we can do this, we must be rid of the outmoded bias of materialistic thought; and we must recognize that different types of studies demand different approaches.

2

The Limitations of the Old Framework

It is obvious to many people today that material science does not satisfy the deeper needs of man, no matter how much comfort and ease it may give the body and no matter how much pride it gives the intellect. In constructing a modern science of psychology, we have not only to satisfy the intellect but also to provide something that the heart and soul of man can respond to. We have today reached the point world-wide where man seems to *know* everything and *understand* nothing. It is fine to gather data and to correlate facts statistically, but too great a concentration on particulars puts one out of touch with the integrative, symphonic, coherent power of the whole. We therefore lose the restorative power of the great universal truths. Modern science finds its depth in the details of matter; and a problem arises from the fact that these findings are never re-assembled into a complete and living whole. Since we seem bent upon studying complex phenomena, the simple truths which are changeless are forgotten or derided. As Goethe (1950) writes in *Faust*,

> He who would study organic existence
> First drives out the soul with rigid persistence;
> Then the parts in his hand he may hold and class,
> But the spiritual link is lost, alas!
> (Part I, scene IV, p.66)

Today we need more of an emphasis on the whole rather than merely its parts; we need to look once again at the universal principles underlying all life before we begin to tamper with nature. The ecological crisis that confronts us today is only one obvious result of man's use of "knowledge" without the guidance of wisdom, i.e., an understanding of the underlying pattern of the whole system. In their impatience for quick "results," psychiatrists resort to shock treatment and drugs and call it "therapy," farmers resort to pesticides and chemical fertilizers, justifying their actions as an economic necessity or as a brave attempt to prevent mankind from starving. It is the understanding of universal principles, the harmony of the whole, and the underlying patterns of life that astrology can provide modern man. This is the reason why so many people in the United States are becoming interested in astrology: because they sense in it some power to reveal the order and meaning of their apparently-chaotic lives.

Joseph Goodavage (1967), author of *Astrology: The Space Age Science*, clearly expresses the modern disenchantment with materialistic science:

> It seems we have reached the saturation point with materialism. It has generated nothing but frustration, hatred, wars, and class strife. Its goal is empty and meaningless, a blind alley for humanity. We must admit the existence of new evidence, all of which points unerringly toward the sublime unity and interdependence of everything in nature. (p. 139)

It is, in fact, most striking how many modern scientists and philosophers give recognition to the mental and spiritual aspect of the cosmos. In his book, *The Mysterious Universe*, Jeans (1932) writes:

> Today there is a wide measure of agreement, which on the physical side of science approaches to unanimity, that the stream of knowledge is leading us towards a non-mechanical reality; the universe begins to look more like a great thought than like a great machine. Mind no longer appears as an accidental intruder into the realm of matter; we are beginning to suspect that we ought rather to hail it as the creator and governor of the realm of matter .... The old dualism of mind and matter ... seems likely to disappear; not through matter becoming in any way more shadowy or insubstantial than heretofore, or through mind becoming resolved into a function of the working of matter, but through substantial matter resolving itself into a creation and manifestation of mind. We discover that the universe shows evidence of a designing or controlling power that has something in common with our own individual minds — not, so far as we have discovered, emotion, morality, or aesthetic appreciation, but the tendency to think in the way which, for want of a better word, we describe as Mathematical ....

Many people are today attracted to astrology because it reveals that "designing power" of the universe within a mathematical framework.

Irving F. Laucks (1971) explains that the "God is Dead" philosophy of modern times arises from the fact that the *material*

God is dead, an event that we should all welcome since it makes room for the birth of a new, more complete view of life and the universe:

> Oriental religions were less materialistic in their ideas. In order to create the world, they used a concept which today could easily conform to all we know about "energy." Since Western science has finally found that energy is a more basic force than matter from which to construct a universe, in this respect Western science and Oriental religions might well cooperate.
>
> Again, in existence beyond death Oriental religions are non-materialistic. Either their concepts of reincarnation or of Nirvana after death could well agree with "energy" as a future medium of existence, rather than of space, time and matter, as Western religions have taught.
>
> This idea that "matter" of which this great universe is composed ... is nothing but an intangible thing such as we call a force or "energy" is perhaps the most important concept ever formed by the youthful brain of man. To science this idea is less than a century old, and neither science nor the public has yet begun to grasp its full import. (p. 4)

This new emphasis on "energy" as a more fundamental reality than matter is considered in detail in Part II of this book and in Appendix B, particularly the relation of energy concepts to astrology.

In daily life, the spiritual side of man is inseparable from man's psychological life. The very derivation of the word "psychology" reveals how closely the mind of man is interrelated with his spiritual nature. The Greek word *psyche* originally had two meanings. The first meaning is best translated as *soul*, i.e., the deepest source of life within man. The second meaning was *butterfly*, which had the connotation of the immortal spirit pervading all of nature and each individual human being. Since then, *psyche* has been defined largely as "mind," although many experimental and physiological psychologists would like to eliminate even so immaterial a term as that. (According to the psychological and spiritual sciences of India, however, the mind and the soul, while they are closely intertwined in the daily functioning of most people's lives, are in reality totally distinct. One of the main tenets of advanced forms of yoga is the idea that the soul can be free only when it is no longer enslaved to the mind.)

Fortunately for psychology, some humanistic psychologists are not so shy of taking into account the inner-most aspects of man's life, those dimensions of man which transcend merely intellectual-mental activities. A psychology based upon observable behavior, assuming that only "objective" data is worthwhile, is really no psychology at all. To restrict the domain of psychology to the laboratory study of animals and to the overt behavior patterns of human beings is inconsistent with the definition of the supposed object of study: the *psyche* itself, that mind-soul-spirit quality that pervades all human endeavors and perhaps all of creation. As Jung points out repeatedly in his writings, we can't be "objective" when we study the psyche of man; for we have to study the psyche through the psyche of the observer. This can be considered a criticism of all so-called objective research; but it is surely most relevant to the study of man himself and the workings of his inner life. The fad of "objective" studies in psychology, particularly the behavioral school, ignores the basic fact of human uniqueness: creativity. As the research of both Jung and the child psychologist Jean Piaget have shown, the mind operates not as a passive mirror but rather as an active and purposeful artist. To quote once again from Rudin's book (1968) *Psychotherapy and Religion:*

> Modern-day psychology cannot afford, as did that of the nineteenth century, to bypass the pressing current questions concerning the soul and to lock itself up in a laboratory of apparatus in order to conduct experiments emulating those of chemistry and physics. Psychology cautiously enters into life, into the uninterrupted process of the individual soul, into its ups and downs, pouring light into its secret desires and longings .... (p. 21)

In a similar vein, psychologist O. Hobart Mowrer (1969) has written that "... this matter of man's total adjustment and psycho-social survival does not quickly yield up its innermost secrets to conventional types of scientific inquiry ..." (p. 14). This fact explains why the psychology of the twentieth century has for the most part grown stagnant and remains totally irrelevant to the daily lives and longings of each of us. The only psychologists in recent years who have made strides toward an understanding of man's inner life and immediate experience are those who have ventured outside the restrictive domain of conventional scientific inquiry. I include here those who have begun to research such long-neglected areas as meditation, ESP, Oriental psychology and philosophy, mythology, comparative religion, and the use of astrology and other ancient techniques as psychological tools. All of these areas of study, which could loosely be grouped as aspects of a truly humanistic psychology, have proven useful in our quest for freeing and using creatively the qualities and abilities that are unique to man alone. If our aim in the study of psychology were to develop more efficient techniques of conditioning, brainwashing, and manipulation of our fellowman, then we should concentrate on the behavioral side of man's life. But if we want to use the powerful tool of science in order better to appreciate ourselves and others, to learn to live in a healthy, harmonious way, and to liberate that which is most inspiring and creative within man, then we have to realize the limitations of the materialistic approach and begin to venture into the unknown, supported only by our faith in the wisdom of nature and the high destiny of man.

3

Different Approaches to Knowledge & The Question of Proof

I know the truth only when it becomes life in me.
— Soren Kierkegaard

The physicist-philosopher L. L. Whyte (1948), in his book *The Next Development in Man*, argues that the Western intellectual tradition has been marked by what he calls a "dissociation." What he means by this term is that, increasingly from the time of Plato and St. Paul to the twentieth century, Western man's deliberate behavior, directed by his mind, has been organized through the use of static concepts of nature, while his spontaneous behavior, in direct response to his immediate experience, inevitably continues to express the formative processes which really characterize all nature. This dissociation between the body and mind, the self and nature, the intellect and the feeling-intuitional sense has permeated Western man's approach to all of life: intellectual, religious, economic, and political. The rare exceptions to this trend have usually been poets, mystics, and others on the periphery of socio-cultural life. This dissociative trend has led to the breakdown of Western culture, as seen in the great wars, the present-day ecological crisis, and rapidly increasing physical and mental problems. Whyte (1954) goes on to say:

> If the whole of nature is one great system in perpetual transformation and development, the attempt to isolate any part is bound to lead to failure. In particular the separation of man as subject from the field of objective nature blinds him to the form of life proper to him. Man can only fully understand himself by fusing the objective knowledge which is gained by observation of the whole of organic nature with the subjective knowledge of individual experience. This can bring a new ease and self-acceptance, an innocence based on knowledge. The negative

> prejudices of conventional morality are replaced by a positive
> enthusiasm for developing life .... (p. 121)

Whyte points out that, since the time of the Greeks, thinkers have fallen into two camps, which can be called the Atomistic School and the Holistic School; and the adherents to each approach dislike the other, complementary view. In our daily lives, we use both approaches, with varying degrees of emphasis, although the holistic approach is by far the most comprehensive and useful for understanding vast systems or organic wholes; for, as Whyte writes, the holistic approach (i.e., a consciousness of form and pattern) cannot be ignored since *it is an irrefutable fact that regular forms dominate nature and everything we see and experience.*

This same problem of conflicting views of life is noted by the existential philosophers and psychologists. Psychologist Rollo May (1958) says that existentialism "seeks to understand man by cutting below the cleavage between subject and object by which the Western mind had been bedeviled since shortly after the Renaissance." Many existentialists recognize at least two different approaches to understanding: that of "mystery" (which Gabriel Marcel refers to as all that may be labeled personal, both human and divine) and that of "problem" (which arises from the *analysis* of parts of the whole). Marcel goes on to say that existence itself is not "explained" but rather has to be "illuminated" in order to gain real understanding. The French philosopher Pascal denied that the world and especially man could be truly understood by means of rational analysis. He asserted that intuition, i.e., seeing through the surface of things into their essential mystery, was ultimately the key for understanding man and the world. What Marcel and Pascal are referring to here is today called the "holistic" approach. Let us elucidate here the basic differences of approach which led to the dissociation in Western man and to the misplaced emphasis on purely intellectual functioning.

The great mystery schools of antiquity (the predecessors of modern psychotherapeutic techniques) taught that the human consciousness is limited only by the arbitrary intellectual boundaries which it imposes upon itself. When studying the history of

Western civilization, we always find that the Greeks' emphasis on science and reason is considered the crucial turning point in Western man's intellectual and cultural development. This era was of course one of great growth in man's understanding of himself and the universe. However, the contribution of the Greeks was not limited to the discovery of certain natural laws active in the material world; it also extended into the realm of the individual's inner life and growth. "Know thyself" was the key idea underlying the development of Greek philosophy; and the word "philosophy" (*philosophia*) literally means "love of wisdom." Science for the Greeks was not merely the collection of data in the hope that certain correlations could be discovered. It was rather a systematic search for the *essential* truths underlying life and nature, and an attempt to discover not only *natural* laws but also the *universal* metaphysical laws of life itself. And, for the Greeks, "reason" did not refer merely to the computer-like calculations of the logical mind, but rather to an inspired (or "inspirited") combination of analysis and intuition founded upon ideals of elegance and symmetry.

Many modern scientists still believe that the most comprehensive theories necessarily have to be the most elegant, aesthetically satisfying, and essentially simple. However, for many scientists, this ideal has been forgotten or derided; and the search for comprehensive truths has been neglected due to an overemphasis on critical analysis. To be truly scientific, one has to abstain as much as possible from imposing his own expectations, desires, and preconceived intellectual boundaries on men's minds, in order that the human spirit can grow freely and flower. Most scientists, however, including psychologists, have unnecessarily limited their view of man and his potentials. When a man intellectually builds a wall around himself, it does not affect what is outside the wall; it merely prevents the man from seeing what is outside and it distorts the structure of the whole. We try to understand life by limiting it and categorizing it, primarily on the basis of our intellectual prejudices and emotional predispositions. But all too often, we wind up merely limiting ourselves; for what is, no matter what we may say about it, *is*. Our culture's educational institutions could learn a profitable lesson from Zen Master Shunryu Suzuki-roshi (1970):

"Beginner's mind" is our original mind, actually an empty and ready mind. If our mind is empty, it is always ready for anything; it is open to everything. In the beginner's mind there are many possibilities; in the expert's there are few. . . . In the beginner's mind there is no thought, "I have attained something." All self-centered thoughts limit our vast mind. When we have no thought of achievement, no thought of self, we are true beginners. Then we can really learn something.

The intellect is mainly useful for utilizing the outer, material world. We see a clear example of this fact when we note how Western science and technology boomed shortly after the goddess of reason was enthroned in Europe. But it is equally true that we have seen no such boom in our understanding of man himself through the efforts of materialistic psychology. It has been only recently, when reason and intellect have been balanced by an emphasis on experience, feeling, and intuition, that some branches of psychology have begun to make progress in the understanding of man's inner nature. Until now, the application of purely intellectual analysis to the understanding of the inner world of experience has not been able to prove or disprove anything about the ultimate philosophical or religious questions of life which form the foundation of anyone's psychological structure. Logical positivism is the extreme manifestation (and logical result) of the analytical approach, which may be said to be aiming at a maximum of abstraction with a minimum of meaning. And it is *meaning* that man needs; and an understanding of man's need for meaning is necessary to any psychology of health and wholeness. Meaning is provided from within, not from without; hence, the analytical approach alone can never help man to fulfill his deepest needs.

Psychologist Wilson Van Dusen (1967) expresses basically the same idea:

All this becomes more reasonable if the world is no longer viewed as the physicist's abstract, objective world — a totally impersonal other-than-one's self. That world is a conceptual construction convenient to physics but grossly inaccurate in the psychology of persons. The personal world, the only one each of us really knows, is the world painted in the tones of all one's own personal meanings. The world shuts off when I sleep. Its time slows down when I am bored and accelerates when I am involved . . . . The world of persons is a personal world.

> Lightning and thunder are beautiful to me. Are they something
> else to you? Where is the objective impersonal lightning and
> thunder? They are part of the "reported events" which don't
> mean much to a person. The impersonal objective world is the
> one no one cares about! (p. 233)

French biologist and anthropologist Père Teilhard de Chardin
(1936) also questions the validity of so-called "objective" knowledge:

> Truth is simply the complete coherence of the universe in rela-
> tion to every point contained within it. Why should we be sus-
> picious of or underestimate this coherence just because we our-
> selves are the observers? We hear continually of some sort of
> anthropocentric illusion contrasted with some sort of objective
> reality. In fact, there is no such distinction. Man's truth is the
> truth of the universe for man; in other words, it is simply truth.

The wholeness and coherence of all life and the oneness of man
and the universe referred to in de Chardin's quotation provides a
concise and elegant theory which supports the approach of traditional geocentric astrology and, in essence, leads to the
microcosm-macrocosm correlation noted by ancient authors.

In order to elucidate how this over-emphasis on "objectivity"
has developed, we should here mention Jung's theory of personality. According to Jung, there are four primary ways of *knowing*,
which Jung calls the four basic psychic functions: thinking, feeling, sensation, and intuition. Thinking and sensation can be
grouped together since analytical thought is based primarily
upon data from the outer world received through the senses. Intuition and feeling can also be grouped together since these functions arise from *within* the individual and are not totally conditioned by the socio-cultural milieu of the time. Also, knowledge
gained through intuition and feeling is subjective and personal,
in the sense that it can't be proved or objectively verified. (Since
these four functions can be grouped into two distinct approaches
to knowledge, I will henceforth speak of "thinking" and "intuition" to indicate the two groups.) The thinking faculty functions
through the systematic classification and discrimination of facts
which are then arranged in certain patterns according to the type
of logic employed. ("Logic," needless to say, is markedly different
for different people.) The faculty of intuition, on the other hand,

reveals to the individual an immediate insight into, and perception of, the workings of the whole system being considered. Intuition is basically man's power of direct perception and immediate knowledge which circumvents, transcends, or penetrates through the slower workings of the logic-bound intellect. Modern science has completely overlooked the intuitive function in man, perhaps assuming that "intuition" is merely thought prejudicially colored by personal feelings. But, in reality, intuition is a type of fully conscious perception, whereas "feeling" emanates from vague, unconscious roots. The intuitive function is closely related to the aesthetic function in man; for the wholeness of perception seen in great art arises from the intuitive perception of order and harmony and from an inner knowledge that is arrived at by means transcending rational thought. By the very nature of intuition, the language of art is more suited to its expression than are abstract theories or mathematics. As L.L. Whyte (1954) writes in *Accent on Form:*

> Intuitive awareness, expressed in nonverbal form, comprises a greater range of experience than the verbal and algebraic symbols of language and mathematics can yet convey. (p. 122)

The great German poet Goethe (1954) expressed his preference for the comprehensiveness of intuitive perception in this way: "I should like to speak like Nature, altogether in drawings." In constructing a psychology that deals chiefly with persons and personal experience, the intuitional faculty is of prime importance; for, as psychologist Wilson Van Dusen (1967) writes, "I would have no quarrel with anyone who asserted the language of the novelist, poet, or musician is closer to the quality of human experience than the language of psychologists." We should add to this quotation the fact that the symbolic language of astrology is also closer to the quality of human experience than the usual language of psychologists.

In trying to understand the faculty of intuition, we must realize that the imaginative and intuitive activities of the human mind are not mere by-products of analysis and sense-dominated logic. For we see that the truly creative people often threaten the very social order, values, and ways of thinking that gave them birth. Hence, if these people do not gain their insights through training in the established social institutions and through socio-cultural patterns, where does this creativity come from? We must answer that the intuitive function in man is the prime source of all new insights and imagination. The intellect is conditioned by many factors, but the intuition (the portal of inspiration) seems to have relative freedom.

Let us here clarify the distinction between the different approaches to knowledge:

		Thinking	*Intuition*
a)	assumption	: causality	not necessarily causal (correspondences within the whole)
b)	aim	: discrimination & classification	synthesis & order
c)	nature of resulting concepts	: static	process & orderly change
d)	way of proceeding	: systematic	all-at-once-ness (synchronistically)
e)	language	: quantitative (mathematics or precise words)	qualitative (feeling, visual, artistic)
f)	orientation	: problem	mystery
g)	field of study	: contents & details of whole system	whole system and the form & pattern of the whole
h)	units of language	: signs	symbols
i)	domain of usefulness	: outer world (material)	inner world (psychic, spiritual)

It appears from the above that, whereas intellect can reveal the secrets of outer life and the workings of matter, it is intuition that can reveal the secrets of inner life and the field of personal experience. The ideal for a comprehensive science of the psyche would be a fusion of the two; but in a psychology that takes as its main field of study the inner life of man and the meaning of his experience, the intuitive function must not only have a place but indeed must be accepted as the primary approach toward a deep and satisfying understanding of the individual person. This is so because the subjective experience of persons is by its very nature *qualitative*. The analytical thinking approach already has the quantitative language of mathematics to describe its findings; but the intuitive approach until now has had no generally-accepted and comprehensive language to represent the qualitative findings in its domain.

Astrology is just this language which is so necessary to describe human experience and uniqueness in a useful and comprehensive way. Although only a small percentage of the academic and scientific establishment accepts astrology as the answer to this need (if indeed they recognize the need at all), a large segment of the general population has naturally gravitated toward astrological ways of seeing things and understanding their experience. In other words, astrology can be for the healing arts (medicine, psychology, psychiatry, etc.) what the periodic table is for chemistry. Zipporah Dobyns (1971), a psychologist who is working toward the integration of astrology and psychology and who uses astrology as the primary tool in her practice, calls astrology "man's greatest glimpse of the unifying order in the cosmos successfully translated into cognitive conceptual form." She goes on to say:

> ... it seems there are two master languages which have universal application as ways to classify and symbolically describe reality. The language of quantity we call mathematics can be used to describe anything that can be counted or measured. I would like to suggest astrology as the most universally useful language of quality. ... I am quite sure that before many more years have passed, the myriad personality systems now competing in modern psychology will quietly disappear, and be replaced by a purified and unified astrology. In the end, this is inevitable, for astrology provides the only system in which there are external referents for the categories which are visible, predictable, and capable of complexity infinitely beyond any personality classification devised by psychology. (p. 8)

The two different approaches to knowledge naturally give rise to two different kinds of proofs: statistical (or "objective") and experiential (also called "existential"). Let us here briefly examine the whole question of "proof" in relation to astrology.

Proofs of Astrology: Why & How

Although many modern astrologers (as well as non-astrologers) are conducting statistical studies of astrological premises, we must realize that we cannot count on a statistical approach to explain everything; for many areas of experience and *qualities* inherent in life are not amenable to such a study. In fact, even when a statistical study does reveal correlations of great significance, they often still do not "explain" the operation of the phenomenon itself. For example, there are certain "empirical laws" in science which are found by experiment to be true but for which no rational explanation has so far been provided. The best example of such laws in astronomy is what is known as "Bode's Law." This relates to the distances of planets from the sun. If we write a series of numbers: 0, 3, 6, 12, 24, 48, 96, and if we then add 4 to each term, we get 4, 7, 10, 16, 28, 52, 100. Bode's Law states that the distances of the planets are in the ratio of these numbers; that is, if the distance of Mercury from the Sun is taken as four units, that of Venus from the sun is seven, Earth ten units, Mars sixteen, Jupiter fifty-two and Saturn one hundred. The figure twenty-eight originally had no known referent until the asteroids were discovered. By extending the law beyond one hundred, astronomers were able to predict the existence of Uranus, Neptune, and Pluto. The appearance of these trans-saturnian planets at the mathematically-appointed time and place forms one of the most thrilling chapters in the history of scientific discoveries. And this achievement is largely due to the intuitive perception of Bode, to which no analytical basis has been provided to this day. Hence, we must be cautious when we use statistical methods, lest our expectations of such an approach exceed its field of utility.

The primary limitation of the statistical method is that, while it is useful for dealing in generalizations, groups, and quantities, it is almost always rather irrelevant in relation to individuals and qualities, which are the primary focal points of a person-centered psychology or astrology. As psychologist Rollo May (1969) writes:

> . . . if you take individuals as units in a group for the purpose of statistical prediction — certainly a legitimate use of psychologi-

cal science — you are exactly *defining out of the picture* the characteristics which make this individual an existing person. Or when you take him as a composite of drives and deterministic forces, you have defined for study everything except *the one to whom these experiences happen,* everything except the existing person himself. (p. 372)

Astrology is unique in that it includes both the aspect of wholeness and art, and that of details, precision, and science. But, as Dane Rudhyar (1964) writes, the emphasis is on "the art of interpreting the cyclic ebbs and flows of the basic energies and activities of life so that the existence of an individual person . . . is seen as an ordered process of change, a process which has inherent meaning and purpose." Rudhyar (1968) goes on to say that the measurements in astrology are symbolic and have to be translated into human *qualities*:

> You cannot measure quantitatively the love, the response to beauty, the character of a person — not unless you make of that person a computer-like machine; and this is what our present-day science is trying to make of individual persons.

Astrology deals essentially with, in Rudhyar's words, "a quality of being," and it is just such a qualitative language that transcends the domain of statistical studies.

The psychologist C.G. Jung has also written about the limitations of the statistical viewpoint. In his book *The Undiscovered Self,* Jung (1958) says:

> The statistical method show the facts in the light of the ideal average but does not give us a picture of their empirical reality. While reflecting an indisputable aspect of reality, it can falsify the actual truth in a most misleading way. This is particularly true of theories which are based on statistics. The distinctive thing about real facts, however, is their individuality. Not to put too fine a point on it, one could say that the real picture consists of nothing but exceptions to the rule, and that, in consequence, absolute reality has predominantly the character of *irregularity*.

> Scientific education is based in the main on statistical truths and abstract knowledge and therefore imparts an unrealistic, rational picture of the world, in which the individual, as a merely marginal phenomenon, plays no role. The individual, however, as an irrational datum, is the true and authentic carrier of reality, the *concrete* man as opposed to the unreal ideal or normal man to whom the scientific statements refer.

We ought not to underestimate the psychological effect of the statistical world picture: it displaces the individual in favor of anonymous units that pile up into mass formations. (p. 17 ff.)

The fact that astrology provides us with *unique formulations and combinations of general, archetypal qualities* gives it its eminent place as the ideal psychological tool. Although astrology does deal with archetypal principles (see Chapter 4), it also provides through the birth-chart a comprehensive symbol of human uniqueness and individuality. In fact, the reason that most astrology still uses a geocentric structure is that the earth-centered and person-centered aspects of astrological work are emphasized far more than any supposed "objective" framework. Although astrology has been criticized for this seeming misrepresentation, the fact remains that, for people living on the planet Earth, the earth *is* the center of their world, just as the individual is the center of his personal world.

The validity of astrology can be demonstrated most clearly by a type of proof which is relevant to its intrinsic character. The real question to be answered in any inquiry into astrology is whether, and to what extent, astrology is significant and of essential value to human beings, and, in the domain of psychology, whether astrology is helpful to the psychologist and to the client. Any other question of "proving" astrology is purely academic. When we see an increasing number of psychologists and psychiatrists, as well as a large percentage of the general public, using astrology and finding in it something of great value to them, we must assume that it is indeed "useful." To those who *know* the value of such a technique, the question of proving or disproving astrology never arises. In psychology particularly, the actual practitioners of various types of psychotherapy have for the past forty years always been years ahead of the theoreticians; so we should not expect the scientific and academic establishment to come up with "proofs" for the validity of astrological premises. For the sake of completeness, Appendix A lists statistical and scientific studies that have bearing on astrology. But there is yet another kind of proof, which astrologer-philosopher Dane Rudhyar calls "existential proof."

According to Rudhyar (1970), only an "existential proof" can be relevant to truly individual situations:

> An existential proof cannot be based on general categories. It can only derive from the personal experience of an individual in a particular situation involving a complex, and never *exactly* duplicated, set of relationships. If the situation produces results significant for an individual, then it must be considered valid for this individual. If, after having studied astrology and his exactly-calculated birth chart, a person for the first time realizes that the sequence of his life-events, which had so far seemed to him utterly chaotic and purposeless, makes sense — if as a result of his study, he is able to feel a direction and purpose inherent in his life as an individual, and how he had been blocking this realization of meaning, orientation, and purposefulness — then astrology is "existentially proven" to be effective in this particular case. (p. 7)

To many modern astrologers, the attempt to make of astrology just one more science of the traditional type, i.e., to establish statistical correlations upon a purely causal framework, would mean the sacrifice of much in astrology that is unique and deeply significant. In fact, according to this view, to do so would necessitate the neglect of the holistic, cosmic framework from which astrology derives its usefulness and comprehensiveness. Those who seek to create a modern science of astrology (that is, to formulate it in such a way that it would be acceptable to the critical, materialistic mind) are overlooking the fact that astrology's greatest strength comes from its being the most comprehensive and universally-applicable cosmic language known to man. The "scientific" aspect of astrology surely exists with regard to precision of measurement. But that is only the raw material for the *art* of astrology; and it is this art, this technique of creatively applying the scientific factors, that can never be understood in a statistically-based, objectively-verifiable astrology. Not only would much of the subtlety of astrology be eliminated, but the deeper meanings to which the soul of man responds would be absent. As Anna Crebo (1970) writes, to try to do so would be "attempting to force a cosmic language to express itself within the framework of our present limited concepts. It is possible that this language is translatable to us only in terms of 'images, visual relations, gestures, qualities.' " (p. 81)

The Swiss physician Alexander Ruperti (1971) expresses a similar opinion:

> Unfortunately, the scientific attitude has tended to increase the chaos at the psychological level, because it destroys the value of the individual and because the type of city and machine-controlled existence it has produced has also destroyed man's sense of participation in the rhythms of life and nature. Modern man tends to forget that science's main concern is the establishment of collective laws for general application only. The environment science offers to man does not present him with any *human* meaning or purpose; merely cold, intellectual facts which are supposed to be unchangeable but which, from any long perspective, may easily change according to the rhythm of vast cosmic cycles.
>
> What is the value of trying to fit astrology into the straight-waistcoat of scientific knowledge, when its technique and basic philosophy enable one to escape from the prison into which science has put man's mind? Would it not be more worthwhile for us to build up astrology on *its own* foundations and thus present it as a means to *complement* the scientific emphasis and to re-orient the consciousness and thinking of our modern civilization which has lost contact with its vital roots in the creative rhythms of life? ... Science gives us knowledge, nothing more. It has nothing to say concerning the why of the universe, and everything dealing with the understanding and the significance of individual human values and goals is outside its domain. ... astrology's gift to mankind is its capacity to solve and explain that which science cannot and does not attempt to do. We need more vision, more constructive imagination, if we would free ourselves from our present bondage to analytical and mathematical details, to statistical methods. The whole is always more than the sum of its parts and no collection of separate data, however complete, on the outward behavior and characteristics of a person, will ever reveal him as a living human being with a life purpose of his own. (p. 7)

Before we can more deeply appreciate the role of astrology in a newly-formulated psychology, we must examine the universal and archetypal factors which underly all life and influence all attempts to understand experience.

4

Archetypes & Universal Principles

*Earthly things must be known to be loved: divine
things must be loved to be known.*
— Pascal

The true purpose of philosophy (before "philosophy" came to be merely a sterile word game used to perpetuate intellectual arrogance) was once held to be the search for essences and for the underlying nature of manifested things, all based upon a love of wisdom. In modern terms, this could be called a search for the archetypal level of reality. Nowadays, of course, any statement about "essences" would cause one to be labeled an "occultist." But when we look around us at the world and try to make some sense of our lives and the sort of reality with which the mass media deals, we have to admit that everything of significance is occult, that is, hidden. Despite all the supposed knowledge that we have accumulated, *meaning* is nowhere to be found, except in those fields of study that point to a unity between man and the universe. This unity of, and relation between, man and the universe is really the only assumption upon which astrology is based.

The field of comparative religion and mythology is one discipline which clearly points to an abiding unity in all life. This is not the place to examine in detail the contributions of C.G. Jung in this field, for his collected works represent a lifetime of scholarly study and demanding research. Suffice it to say that, more than anyone else, C.G. Jung showed beyond any doubt that the primary life-motivating agents in the individual psyche and the overall psychological patterns in entire cultures are manifestations of "archetypal" factors in the human psyche. These archetypes are inherent in the psychological layer of life. Jung calls this psychic substratum the "Collective Unconscious" and describes the archetypes as the universal principles underlying and motivating all psychological life, individual and collective. In both astrology and mythology these universal principles constitute the main field of study, the difference between them being that, whereas mythology places its emphasis on the cultural *manifestations* of the archetypes in various patterns, astrology utilizes the *essential archetypal principles themselves* as its language for understanding the fundamental forces and patterns in both individual and cultural life. There is historically a strong interrelationship between the myths of a particular culture and the type of astrology it has developed. In fact, astrology can be viewed as the most comprehensive mythological framework that has ever arisen in human culture. As mentioned in the prologue to this book, myth ideally serves as a vitalizing force in any culture by showing man's relationship to a larger, more universal reality. The fact that Western culture no longer has any viable mythology to energize it explains in part why astrology has seen a definite rebirth in recent years; for people have always needed a pattern of growth and order to guide their collective lives and to infuse their individual experience with meaning. As Joseph Campbell (1960) writes:

> Whence the force of these insubstantial themes, by which they are empowered to galvanize populations, creating of them civilizations, each with a beauty and self-compelling destiny of its own? And why should it be that whenever men have looked for something solid on which to found their lives, they have chosen, not the facts in which the world abounds, but the myths of an immemorial imagination . . .? (p. 20)

The most obvious answer to Cambell's questions is that the gods of mythology (just like the planets in astrology) represent *living* forces and principles in the universe and in the lives of each of us. The conclusions drawn from Jung's research into the archetypal foundations of the human mind would lead us to this answer, as would recent studies in comparative religion and in some areas of humanistic psychology. It is my view that astrology provides us with the key to understanding these basic forces and functions in all men by virtue of its being the most comprehensive — and yet at the same time precise — language of energy known to man. As Campbell (1960) writes:

> For it is a fact that the myths of our several cultures work upon us, whether consciously or unconsciously, as energy-releasing, life-motivating, and directing agents . . . . (p. 20)

As man's needs undergo periodic transformations, so his myths must change to suit his new dimension of being. As man's consciousness evolves, so must his myths:

> For, just as in the visible world of the vegetable and animal kingdoms, so also in the visionary world of the gods: there has been a history, an evolution, a series of mutations, governed by laws. (Campbell, 1960, p. 21)

Just as man's understanding of his gods and religions has changed, although they still continue to exist in some form or another, so astrology still exists as well as man's need for it, despite all the attempts to rationalize it out of existence. But we must re-evaluate our approach to it, seeing it not simply as a pattern of celestial clues to our immutable fate, as it has been traditionally viewed, but rather utilizing it as a way of understanding our fundamental nature, discovering our place in the universe, and helping us to live in a creative and fulfilling way. In other words, astrology can be seen as a *consciously usable mythology*. Contemporary Western man has evolved to the point where he is no longer satisfied by living unconsciously according to outmoded myths, rigid dogma, or archaic traditions. But he has gone too far in trying to free himself from limitations and traditions. He has lost touch with the archetypal foundations of his being and with the source of support and spiritual-psychological nourishment which they provide. Astrology can be used as a way of reuniting man with his innermost self, with nature, and with the evolutionary process of the universe.

Universal Principles

> Multa renascentur, quae jam cecidere cadentque, Quae nunc sunt in honore . . . .
> (Much will rise again that has long been buried, and much become submerged which is held in honor today.)
> — Horace

What are these "universal principles" to which we've been referring? By definition, they border on the transcendant since they give rise to all manifestations and observable patterns in the material universe. Many scientists have come to believe that there is an invisible organizing pattern *within* living things, a sort of psychological pattern which guides and determines the form that energy will assume. This tendency toward patterns in nature can be seen in everything from evolutionary theory to the fairly predictable patterns of human physical and psychological development. Another word commonly used to describe this structural phenomenon is "form." The physicist-philosopher L.L. Whyte has written an important book called *Accent on Form* (1954) which deals with what he calls the "formative principles" in all life. In fact, he says that "the most comprehensive natural law expresses a formative tendency" (p. 137).

"Form" is one of man's oldest ideas. The Greeks had numerous theories of perfect forms, from Plato's eternal forms to Euclid's quantitative relations in space to Pythagoras' study of number and geometry. In the Middle Ages, each class of things was said to possess an essence (*essentia* or *quidditas*); and that essence was considered to be not a static quality but rather a source of activity. The deepest reality was seen to be composed of innumerable essences, and the task of philosophy was to apprehend those essences. The essence of anything was the ground of the thing's being, that which makes the thing what it is. And, for the Medieval philosophers, the forms observable in nature were not static entities, but incarnate ideas, in the sense of Plato's *idea* (Carré, 1949). The source of these eternal ideas was seen as the "universal mind," the domain and repository of the essences (or "archetypes") of all forms that could ever exist and of all ideas that could ever be thought. (The Universal mind, incidentally, is similar in many ways to Jung's conception of the "Collective Unconscious".) Modern physics, oddly enough, finds itself returning to such long-derided ideas; for what we see, we are now told, is only the outward form (or "wave form") of the underlying reality of vibration and energy. The material "particle" has become an extended pattern; the material atom is now seen as a field of energy. Perhaps there is now once again a need for such a concept as the universal mind, that which actively shapes all forms.

A study of form can perhaps reveal how formless energy is organized into functional wholes; and perhaps it can shed light upon these elusive essences within all things. L.L. Whyte (1954) states that "to understand anything one must penetrate sufficiently deeply toward this ultimate pattern" (p. 28). This is true because the formal pattern seems to determine the properties of its constituents, rather than the other way around, a fact which gives great support to a holistic approach to life. As Whyte (1954) writes, "In an atomistic universe how can regular forms develop? Would they not be at best highly improbable?" (p. 50). According to Whyte, a new understanding of the formative principles of the universe would not only help us to understand the theories of physics, biological organization, and the workings of the mind; but also they can provide man with a serenity that can be achieved in no other way.

> For at this point the Western tradition recognizes the validity of an ancient doctrine of the East; the universal principle has to be valued above any particular expression, if serenity is to be achieved.

> The time has come for a new elegance: a unity of process seen in all particular forms and reconciling their differences. A fresh stress must be laid on universal principles in order to restore a proper equilibrium. (p. 191)

It is just this unity of process seen in all particular forms that astrology provides man. In astrology, every individual is considered a *whole and unique expression of universal principles, patterns, and energies.* The Zodiac was considered by ancient astrologers and philosophers as the "soul of nature," that which gives form and order to life. Astrology is a language of universal principles, a way of perceiving form and order in the life of an individual person, a way of symbolizing each individual's oneness with universal factors. A modern approach to astrology cannot be based on the assumption that an individual human being is "merely" the sum total of universal forces which constitute his psycho-physical makeup; rather the individual is a unique form expressing a unique relationship of universal factors.

As L.L. Whyte (1954) states, "everything in this universe bears some relation to our own nature, its needs and potentialities. Every process mirrors some process in ourselves and evokes some emotion, though we may not be aware of it" (p. 31). Whyte's idea expresses what the ancient astrologers called the relationship between the microcosm and the macrocosm, i.e., the conception that the functions and factors within the individual reflect — or at least correspond with — universal processes and principles. In modern terms, we would say that, since the universe is one whole process ("universe" means *turning of the one*) and consists of innumerable interpenetrating fields of energy, the energy field of any individual man is related intimately to the larger energy field of his cosmic environment. One of astrology's greatest values is that, through an understanding of the universal factors operating in each of us, we can attain a greater understanding of the universal principles of life itself. Science today accepts fingerprints, cardiographs, and encephalographs as useful tools, all of which are relatively unique manifestations of human energies and rhythms. The astrological birth-chart is the graph through which the cosmos (or the larger whole) enables us to understand its energies and rhythms, particularly how they operate within each individual.

In psychology, the main body of work that deals with universal principles and formative principles is that of Dr. Carl Jung. Jung's "archetypes" are not physical structures, but rather, according to Jung (1959),

> ... might perhaps be compared to the axial system of a crystal, which, as it were, preforms the crystalline structure in the mother liquid, although it has no material existence of its own .... The Archetype in itself is empty and purely formal, nothing but a *facultas praeformandi*, a possibility of representation which is given *a priori*. (pp. 79-80)

Jung goes on to say that "... it seems to me probable that the real nature of the archetype is not capable of being made conscious, that it is transcendent" (p. 81). Edward Whitmont (1970), a Jungian psychiatrist, has written of the Jungian archetypes as "dynamic transpsychological, hence transcendental energy configurations." Dr. Whitmont speaks of "archetypal fields" related to the astrological symbols of the planets and defines the archetypes as "universal, cosmic form patterns and dynamics." Hence, it is clear that the archetypes are identical with the formative principles mentioned by Whyte, and that astrological factors represent these very realities.

If the archetypes are the foundation of all psychic life, and if they are indeed transcendent in themselves (i.e., too subtle or immaterial for immediate conscious apprehension), then it is especially important that we have a language to describe — or at least to point toward — their reality. And, if we can't know these realities in themselves, we can at least understand *how* they function and what they mean to us by studying the only science that deals with such forces: astrology. No matter what label might be used to designate these universal principles, whether archetypes, essences, or formative principles, the fact remains that such forces exist in the universe and influence each of us both from within and from without. This is the reason why some psychologists, psychiatrists, and counselors have recently begun to use astrology as their primary tool for understanding the inner dynamics of their clients. Jung has said that he used astrology in many of his cases, especially with those people whom he had difficulty understanding:

> As I am a psychologist, I'm chiefly interested in the particular light the horoscope sheds on certain complications in the character. In cases of difficult psychological diagnosis I usually get a horoscope in order to have a further point of view from an entirely different angle. I must say that I have very often found that the astrological data elucidated certain points which I otherwise would have been unable to understand.
>
> (from a letter to Prof. B.V. Raman; Sept. 6, 1947)

In an interview with the editor of a French astrological magazine, Jung (1954) stated:

> One can expect with considerable assurance that a given well-defined psychological situation will be accompanied by an analagous astrological configuration. Astrology consists of configurations symbolic of the collective unconscious which is the subject matter of psychology: the "planets" are the gods, symbols of the powers of the unconcscous.

In the same interview, Jung stated that the innate psychic predisposition of an individual "seems to be expressed in a recognizable way in the horoscope." In many of his writings, Jung emphasized that astrology includes the sum total of all ancient psychological knowledge, including both the innate predisposition of individuals and an accurate way of timing life crises:

> I have observed many cases where a well-defined psychological phase or an analagous event has been accompanied by a transit (particularly the afflictions of Saturn and Uranus). (Jung, 1954)

Jungian psychiatrist Edward Whitmont (1970) writes along similar lines:

> Applied in this broader sense, astrological techniques can become as valuable to the depth psychologist as dream interpretation. They would inform him, not of future events or even fixed character traits, but of unconscious basic dynamics and form patterns that a given person is "up against" and to which he continues to react throughout his life in his own peculiar, individual manner as the characteristic way his particular life is embodied in the cosmic whole.

Zipporah Dobyns (1970), a psychologist whom I mentioned earlier, has this to say about astrology's use as a psychological tool:

> It offers, first of all, a personality system based on an external frame of reference which is therefore superior to the arbitrary systems manufactured in such abundance within the field of personality study, and which is almost certain to be the universal system of the psychology of the future. It offers a symbolic blueprint of a human mind and destiny which cannot be manipulated by the subject wishing to "fake good" or "fake bad" as it is relatively easy to do in many psychological questionnaires. It offers insight into areas of which the subject often knows little or nothing . . . repressions, values never consciously verbalized, ambivalences and conflicts projected into events and relationships and never consciously faced. It offers clues to unrealized potentials, talents, natural channels for integration and sublimation, etc. With its record of past and future patterns, it also offers clues to early traumatic events which the depth therapist might wish to explore and to future periods of stress when the individual is likely to need extra support . . . . It permits the "matching" of individuals, from therapist to patient to marriage partners to employee-employer, etc. It is my firm conviction that the psychotherapy or counseling of the future will use the horoscope as routinely as we now use the interview and background data on the subject.

Another psychologist, Ralph Metzner, who has published a book dealing with astrology and related topics called *Maps of Consciousness*, also uses astrology in his practice:

> As a psychologist and psychotherapist, I have been interested in another aspect of this baffling and fascinating subject. We have here a psychological typology and diagnostic assessment device

far exceeding in complexity and sophistication of analysis any existing system. . . . the framework of analysis — the three interlocking symbolic alphabets of zodiac "signs," "houses," and "planetary aspects" — is probably better adapted to the complex varieties of human natures than existing systems of types, traits, motives, needs, factors, or scales.

The system has the additional advantage of being entirely independent of any behavior on the part of the subject, hence free of response bias of any sort . . . . Unlike any other personality assessment device, the astrological pattern has an inherent dynamic: the horoscope interpreted by a skilled and practiced astrologer not only provides a synthetic picture of the person's hereditary inclinations and tendencies, but points to latent potentials, suggests directions of needed growth — in short, gives a symbolic map of the process of self-realization. (Metzner, 1970, pp. 164-165)

Metzner writes in the same article that astrology should be used as "an adjunct of psychology and psychiatry," and he defines astrology as "astronomy applied for psychological purposes."

Only a symbolic language is universal enough (especially one with external referents like astrology) and a-cultural enough to be useful with all people, young and old, rich and poor, from all educational, cultural, and national backgrounds. The great problem with the theories of "personality" in general psychology is that they are only useful for a small segment of any given population. Astrology, on the other hand, is the most complete theory of personality; and it unifies, and provides a foundation for, all the more specialized theories. In addition, whereas symbolic techniques other than astrology may be useful for some people at certain times, they have the disadvantage of lacking external referents and a precise, measurable framework. Astrology actually comprises both the mathematical and the symbolic languages of life, synthesizing both into one harmonic system the uses of which are far broader than any other system, mathematical or symbolic. Astrology proves its comprehensive uniqueness not only by accurately describing types of consciousness, individual differences and uniqueness, and types of energy operating through the person, but in addition it reveals the operation of universal laws of harmonics, polarities, and psycho-physical energies.

5

Approaches to Astrology

Ignotum per ignotius, obscurum per obscurius.
(The unknown through the more unknown, the
obscure through the more obscure.)
— Old Alchemical Dictum

The Causal Approach

The question of "how does astrology work?" can be approached within numerous frameworks. If one sees astrology within a causal framework, there is a large and growing body of evidence to give support to astrology's validity. (See Appendix A.) One of the most common attempts to explain astrology within a causal framework can be called "Cosmic Conditioning," referring to delicately balanced electromagnetic fields within the solar system and within man, which electromagnetic fields are constantly changing as the positions of the planets change. One scientist, Rex Pay (1967), puts it this way:

> Sleeper has pointed out that if the cavity between the earth and ionosphere is regarded as a resonant system, it has a characteristic period of about one-eighth of a second — the time taken for light to travel once around the earth. The resonant frequency is thus about 8 cps., approximatley that of the alpha rhythm of the human brain. Sleeper suggests that the geomagnetic field might provide the fine tuning mechanism for this characteristic frequency. If behavior were affected by changes in this frequency, then the position of the planets might play a larger part in human affairs than previously supposed. (p. 36)

In such a theory, the human nervous system is seen as responsive to the changes in the cosmic environment.

Although at the present time there is no comprehensive and satisfying theory to explain astrology within the framework of causality, the most complete formulation developed so far is that of Glynn (1972). Glynn, who did his doctoral dissertation on electro-magnetic wave theory, maintains that a fully scientific causal explanation of astrology is not far from our grasp. As an interim solution to the problem, he has devised the following hypothetical chain of causality which incorporates all of the scientific data listed in Appendix A. Although, as Glynn states, this is only one possible chain of causation that could be used to explain astrology, such a theory does seem to account for much of the scientific data now assembled on celestial-terrestrial correspondences. The following is his diagram of the theory:

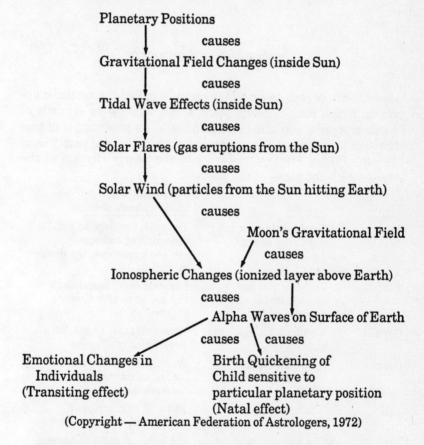

Planetary Positions

causes

Gravitational Field Changes (inside Sun)

causes

Tidal Wave Effects (inside Sun)

causes

Solar Flares (gas eruptions from the Sun)

causes

Solar Wind (particles from the Sun hitting Earth)

causes

Moon's Gravitational Field

causes

Ionospheric Changes (ionized layer above Earth)

causes

Alpha Waves on Surface of Earth

causes   causes

Emotional Changes in
Individuals
(Transiting effect)

Birth Quickening of
Child sensitive to
particular planetary position
(Natal effect)

The "Birth Quickening" mentioned above refers to an idea proposed by Dr. Eugen Jonas of Czechoslovakia. As Glynn says,

Jonas discovered that at the time of birth, the baby is at the peak of his metabolic cycle and actually causes its own birth by releasing adrenalin into the mother's bloodstream. His experiments indicated that this peak always occurs at the same sun-moon angle for each individual. The most logical explanation for this phenomenon is that the embryo has an inherent personality .... The time of birth is then precipitated by the planetary alignments that most strongly influence the baby. Therefore, your birth chart really shows the planetary alignments to which you are most sensitive. (p. 30)

The Symbolic Approach

Another approach to astrology could be called the *symbolic* approach, which considers the planets and signs to be symbols of cosmic processes and universal principles. As an example of this approach to astrology, the following outline is derived partly from Ebertin's (1960) attempt to correlate the yearly rhythm of the seasons with the signs of the zodiac.

Sign	Season	Psychological Correspondence
Aries	Germinating time, unfolding energy	The will, the urge to act, the spirit of enterprise, self-consciousness, the desire to lead
Taurus	Invigoration and strengthening, the creation of form	Perseverance, consolidation, the power to shape, sense of form.
Gemini	Vivification, blossom-time	Vivaciousness, versatility, superficiality
Cancer	Fecundation and fertilization	Wealth of feeling, the feeling of fatherhood and motherhood
Leo	The maturity of the seed	The will to create, self-confidence, all offspring
Virgo	The harvest, utilization of what has been grown	Diligence & care, tidiness, a domesticated nature, the critical faculty

Libra	Balance & adjustment in nature's economy	Sense of justice, striving for harmony, communal sense
Scorpio	Life-terminating processes of nature, continuation of life in the seed	Endurance and perseverance, the ruthless struggle for survival
Sagittarius	Wintersleep of nature	Cultivation of the inner or spiritual side of life, hopeful planning for the future
Capricorn	Crystalization of forms in winter	Untiring struggle for self-preservation, patience, attachment to crystalized social forms
Aquarius	Waiting time, before spring	Expectant attitude, good powers of observation, wealth of plans
Pisces	The swelling of the seed in the earth	First stirrings of new life within the remains of the old

The signs of the zodiac have also been symbolically analyzed in regard to their constellational image (e.g., the ram, bull, twins, etc.). All of these approaches can be fruitful; but no matter which approach is taken, one must admit that astrology must answer a great need in man to have lasted so long and to have been elevated to such a high standing in many cultures. The fact that astrology is the most complete symbolic language has been noted by many psychologists, as shown in the quotations in previous chapters. But the question of what these symbols refer to remains unanswered. Symbols are, after all, *symbols* for the very reason that they refer to *living realities* that are inexpressible (at least at the present time) in any other way. Perhaps this question can never be answered. Perhaps man can never express in words the transcendent realities of the cosmos. Still, we can make use of this symbolic language if we consider it to represent universal patterns, principles, and forces, however transcendent such factors may be. Nevertheless, the symbolic approach to astrology is only complete and useful if it is seen within the framework of a *holistic* approach to all of life.

The Holistic Approach

The philosophy of *holism* assumes that the entire universe is one whole system and that, within the great whole, there are lesser wholes whose structures, patterns, and functions correspond completely to those of the greater whole. The astrologers and philosophers of medieval times used the microcosm-macrocosm concept to express this idea: i.e., the whole universe is, in microcosm, within man; and, in turn, the starry patterns in the heavens were seen as the Grand Man or the Cosmic Man. An example of this sort of correlation may be seen in comparing a single atom to our solar system. The atom is a microcosm of the macrocosmic solar system. This same notion was called the "principle of correspondences" by the English metaphysical poets. The important thing about this approach is that, by studying the cycles and patterns in the greater whole (the planets), we can learn about the cycles and patterns within man himself.

The holistic approach does not assume that causality is the ultimate law of the universe; for if indeed the universe is one *whole*, how can anything ultimately *cause* anything else? Rather, the ancient law of correspondences between parts of a whole is a more appropriate way of looking at holistic phenomena. C.G. Jung calls this law of correspondences "synchronicity," an a-causal connecting principle; and, in reference to astrology, he points out that whatever is born or done at a particular moment in time inevitably bears the *qualities* of that moment. Jung uses the example of a connoisseur of wines who can judge merely by a taste the type of grape, the area where it was produced, and the year of vintage. This law of synchronicity explains why the horoscope is drawn for the moment of the individual's first breath, for that is the time when the new-born child begins his *individual* rhythm in tune with the greater whole of all life around him.

Another psychologist, Zipporah Dobyns (1971) explains her view of synchronicity this way:

> I believe that the planets are part of the order of the cosmos primarily, and, as such, their patterns are enormously useful clues to the same order which exists everywhere. I believe that

the role of the planets in maintaining or creating the order is minimal in comparison to their value as a map or blueprint of the order. (p. 8)

This same idea is expressed throughout ancient and modern literature and philosophy. Emerson, for example, writes: "The Laws by which the Universe is organized reappear at every point and will rule it." Lincoln Barnett (1951) further states: "Einstein's objective in the broadest sense is to show that all forms of nature — stars, planets, light, electricity, and possibly even the tiny particles inside the atom — obey the same universal laws." The primary use and value of astrology is the *application* of this knowledge of universal laws in our individual lives.

More than any other modern astrologer or philosopher, Dane Rudhyar has clearly and comprehensively expounded a holistic approach to astrology and, indeed, to psychology, philosophy, and all things that touch upon man as an individual person. During the past fifty years, Rudhyar has published dozens of books and hundreds of articles dealing with astrological, psychological, cultural, and philosophical subjects, the best known of which are *The Astrology of Personality* (1936), *The Practice of Astrology* (1968), *Birth-Patterns for a New Humanity* (1969), *The Planetarization of Consciousness* (1970), and *An Astrological Study of Psychological Complexes and Emotional Problems* (1966). In addition, he has developed what he calls "Humanistic Astrology," a new and modern approach to astrology which is entirely compatible with modern psychological techniques. More than any other person, Rudhyar has presented astrology in a thoughtful and sophisticated way that blends perfectly with the most hopeful insights of modern science, philosophy, and psychology.

The philosophy underlying all of Rudhyar's works is that of *holism*, the basic premise of which is that existence manifests at all levels in terms of *wholes*, i.e., organized fields of interdependent activities. For Rudhyar, astrology is man's most complete language of the form, structure, and rhythm of functional wholes. In one of his earliest books, *The Astrology of Personality* (1936), Rudhyar refers to astrology as an "algebra of life," that is, a way of understanding the order inherent in all life, individual and collective. Furthermore, he has this to say about astrology in one of his more recent works (1969):

> Astrology, when we look closely at what it is able to interpret and give meaning to, appears as a symbolic language in which the structure in space and time of larger wholes (like the solar system) is related to the structural development of lesser wholes (an individual person, or humanity-as-a-whole). Astrology is indeed the practical application of a holistic philosophical approach to existence. According to this philosophy, every existential whole is contained within a greater whole which in turn is a lesser whole contained within a still greater whole. An organized system of existential activities is therefore both the container of lesser wholes, and one of the contents of a greater system. (p. 35)

> Astrology, as I see it, essentially is dealing with cycles of motions and cosmic (or bio-cosmic) rhythms. It is dealing with "form" or gestalt — with structuring principles inherent in every organized system of activities; thus in every whole. It is not a question of literal, direct, external influence exerted by some celestial body upon entities living on this earth. Astrology is a way of studying and understanding the arrangement or organization of a few essential functions and drives in every organized whole of activity. In olden days this concept was expressed as the structural correspondence between microcosm and macrocosm; but originally it was the entire earth which was seen as the microcosm, analogical in basic structure to the whole universe. Only later on, as the process of human individualization proceeded and individual persons emerged from the all-pervading and totally controlling matrices of tribal societies, did such individual persons come to be regarded as microcosms — a fact which Jesus powerfully affirmed when he said: "The Kingdom of heaven is within you." (p. 93)

Even so eminent a scientist as Teilhard de Chardin confirms the value of a holistic approach to life, as, for example, when he writes that the simple can be understood only in terms of the more complex. The psychologist Rollo May (1960) says much the same thing:

> ... it is only a half truth to hold that the organism is to be understood in terms of the simpler elements below it on the evolutionary scale; it is just as true that every new function forms a new complexity which conditions all the simpler elements in the organism. (p. 686)

The Energy Approach

At the present time, the holistic philosophy is for many people the most aesthetically and intellectually satisfying approach to astrology. Yet there is one other approach to astrology which is only now beginning to take clear form and which holds the possibility of resolving many of the differences between advocates of other points-of-view. This approach deals with the essential energies and energy patterns operating through individuals, and these energies are symbolized by the planets and signs in the horoscope. Part II of this book is an attempt to present in a systematic way this approach to astrology, a point of view which focuses upon the fundamental energies which enliven each of us. The energy approach to astrology is in essence a holistic approach, for it incorporates all dimensions of man's life simultaneously. It should be stated at this point, however, that much work is presently under way which sheds light upon the subtle energies within man and the specific *forms of energy* in all of nature. The fact seems clearer all the time that a blind adherence to a purely causal thought framework will never enable us to develop a comprehensive theory of astrology and may even prevent our understanding the proper uses and rationale of astrology. As the Swiss physician-astrologer Alexander Ruperti (1971) writes:

> Where Paracelsus speaks of identity of Macrocosm and Microcosm, where Rudhyar speaks of the principle of sympathetic resonance of all parts of the universal whole, where Jung speaks of a synchronistic principle governing identical manifestations of psychic phenomena in terms of time, modern astrology, because it follows the scientific attitude, insists on *objectifying* such correspondences into a law of cause and effect. In this way, modern astrology betrays its ancient heritage to the fetish of scientific respectability.

> Astrology's true role has been, and should continue to be, that of demonstrating the existence of universal order at the level of development where man's attention is focused at any given time. The time of astrology's usefulness in bringing order to physical plane existence is over. Modern science is far better equipped now for this task than is astrology. But *at the psychological level*, man's nature today is in chaos, and it is for this reason that we suggest that astrology's highest mission, in terms of modern man's crucial needs, is to present a proof of the existence of harmonic order at the psychological level. (p. 6)

6

Humanistic Psychology &
Humanistic Astrology

During the past decade, there has been a resurgence of interest in those aspects of life which are distinctly human and subjective. This approach in psychology has been termed "third force" or "humanistic" psychology, and it is distinctly different from the more mechanistic models of man constructed by previous generations of psychologists. Although Humanistic Psychology is growing at a rapid pace and is increasingly influencing other fields of study, it is still considered by many old-school psychologists to be insufficiently precise and "scientific." Humanistic Psychology is a more comprehensive and holistic approach to man's psychic and emotional life than the majority of other approaches commonly used in the field. Its very comprehensiveness, and its emphasis on holism and subjectivity naturally make the inclusion of easily measurable, objectively-verifiable data more difficult. Still, there is one psychological tool that fulfills Humanistic Psychology's need for a precise system of human types and differences; and that is astrology.

How is Humanistic Psychology different from other approaches to understanding man's nature? First of all, all humanistic psychologists exemplify a trust in the wholeness and potential for growth of each individual person. As psychologist Carl Rogers (1967) writes:

> ... the subjective human being has an importance and a value which is basic: that no matter how he may be labeled or evaluated he is a human person first of all, and most deeply. He is not only a machine, not only a collection of stimulus-response bonds, not an object, not a pawn. (p. 2)

Another psychologist, Maurice Termerlin (1963) writes:

> Unlike scientific goals, the goals of a humanistic psychotherapy are neither predictability nor control. In fact, the more successful psychotherapy is, the less predictable the individual be-

> comes, because his rigidity is reduced and his spontaneity and creativity are increased. (p. 37)

What Termerlin says about Humanistic Psychology might seem to conflict with the emphasis on prediction found in popular ideas about astrology and indeed in some types of astrological practice. Within the scope of a Humanistic Astrology, however, the emphasis is upon the person rather than upon a specific "event." As the foremost spokesman for Humanistic Astrology, Dane Rudhyar, has written, "people happen to events." This is the crucial difference in emphasis between Humanistic Astrology and other uses of astrology. Likewise, the entire emphasis in a humanistic approach to physical or psychological states of "disease" changes from knowing what kind of problem a person has to *what kind of person has a problem.*

Another important new emphasis in Humanistic Psychology is that man's potential for creativity and self-actualization is regarded as more essential than his limitations, abnormalities, and difficulties with social adjustment. In fact, Humanistic Psychology is the only popular approach which allows for man's uniqueness and individual tone of being, the very factors with which astrology deals specifically and exhaustively. The humanistic-existential psychologist Rollo May (1969) defines "being" as the individual's "pattern of potentialities," and he goes on to say that "These potentialities will be shared with other persons but will in every case form a unique pattern in each individual" (p. 371). This quotation from Rollo May could just as easily refer to the individual birth-chart (horoscope), for the astrological birth-chart symbolizes in holistic fashion the unique "pattern of potentialities" which enlivens each of us.

One of the most active promoters of a humanistic approach to psychology is James F.T. Bugenthal, editor of the book *Challenges of Humanistic Psychology*. In an article called "The Challenge That is Man" (1967), Bugenthal writes:

> To make a statement about a distant galaxy is to make a statement about oneself. To propose a "law" of the action of mass and energy is to offer a hypothesis about one's way of being in the world. To write a description of micro-organisms on a slide is to set forth an account of human experience.. . . The humanistic psychologist . . . accepts this basic subjectivism of all experience as his realm of endeavor.

> I mean, very literally, that any statement we make about the
> world (the "out there") is inevitably, inescapably a statement
> about our theory of ourselves (the "in here").. . . The ultimate
> subjectivity of all that we call objective is expressed by many
> writers, from varied backgrounds.. . . The revival of humanistic
> psychology means that scientific attention is once again directed
> toward the primacy of the subjective. (pp. 5-7)

In this quotation, Bugenthal is outlining his vision of the holistic
nature of the universe, which is the basic philosophical premise of
astrology. Bugenthal further describes what he sees as the primary aim of Humanistic Psychology:

> Humanistic psychology has as its ultimate goal the preparation
> of a complete description of what it means to be alive as a
> human being. This is, of course, not a goal which is likely ever to
> be fully attained; yet it is important to recognize the nature of
> the task. Such a complete description would necessarily include
> an inventory of man's native endowment; his potentialities of
> feeling, thought, and action; his growth, evolution, and decline;
> his interaction with various environing conditions . . .; the
> range and variety of experience possible to him; and his mean-
> ingful place in the universe. (p. 7)

Unless he is familiar with the uses and precision of astrology,
Bugenthal is doubtless unaware of how close the achievement of
this goal is. Using astrology as a psychological tool, all of the
points listed in the above quotation can be clarified and sys-
tematized in a comprehensive way, while at the same time maintaining the openness and potential for individual growth that is
so important to a humanistic psychology. Bugenthal also touches
upon the question of predictability:

> . . . humanistic psychology seeks to so describe men and their
> experiences that they will be better able to predict and control
> their *own* experiences (and thus, implicitly, to resist the control
> of others). (p. 11)

This aim is exactly that of Humanistic Astrology, as set forth by
Dane Rudhyar in his voluminous writings. And this predictability does not in any way contradict the premise of man's individual
freedom, for the important and fundamental freedom is to choose
one's own attitude to a given set of circumstances. As the
psychologist Carl Rogers (1967) writes:

It is this inner, subjective, existential freedom which I have observed. It is the burden of being responsible for the self one chooses to be. It is the recognition by the person that he is an emerging process, not a static end product.... A second point in defining this experience of freedom is that it exists not as a contradiction to the picture of the psychological universe as a sequence of cause and effect, but as a complement to such a universe. Freedom, rightly understood, is a fulfillment, by the person, of the ordered sequence of his life. As Martin Buber put it, "The free man ... believes in destiny, and believes that it stands in need of him." He moves out voluntarily, freely, responsibly, to play his significant part in a world whose determined events move through him and through his spontaneous choice and will. Again to quote Buber. "He who forgets all that is caused and makes decisions out of the depths ... is a free man, and destiny confronts him as the counterpart of his freedom. It is not his boundary but his fulfillment."

We are speaking then of a freedom, which exists in the subjective person, a freedom in which the individual chooses to fulfill himself by playing a responsible and voluntary part in bringing about the destined events of his world. This experience of freedom is for my clients a most meaningful development, one which assists them in becoming human, in relating to others, in being a person. (p. 52)

One of the few drawbacks of the humanistic approach to psychology today is that it is attempting to maintain an open, comprehensive attitude toward the individual person without the determining limitations of relative and constantly changing categories, which categories, however, are absolutely necessary in order to attain the descriptive accuracy and theoretical certainty aspired to as Humanistic Psychology's ultimate goal. Hence, we find that much of Humanistic Psychology remains only a set of attitudes or a general approach rather than developing into a precise and useful theory of personality and human growth. Many humanistic psychologists are hesitant to adopt any set of standards or procedures for distinguishing different human types because they have seen that such theories in the past have been used merely to support the social ethic of a particular historical period and eventually degenerate into severe encumbrances in a therapeutic situation. Also, many humanistic psychologists nowadays are actively involved in researching the importance of transcendent, mystical, or "trans-personal" experiences. Such research leads them to confront metaphysical questions and realities; and an acquaintance with that level of experience makes it all the more obvious how insufficient older theories of personality have become. Hence, I feel strongly that the only standard of reference and life-context that is universal enough to provide a foundation for modern humanistic psychology is the universe itself, with its unchanging patterns, cycles, and rhythms.

This is the kind of humanistic astrology that Dane Rudhyar has been developing for the past forty years, an astrology which is person-centered, rather than event-centered, an astrology conceived essentially as a language using the cyclic motions of celestial bodies as symbols which convey to human beings a direct and practically-applicable understanding of the basic patterns which structure individual and collective existence. Such an astrology, i.e., one dealing primarily with form and structure of the whole, provides a meaningful foundation for a psychology which deals mostly with the "contents" of personal experience. Within such a broad context, and seen in perspective against such a universal background, the everyday experiences of normal life and the occasional crises which shape new phases of growth are seen as more understandable and inherently more meaningful. As Rudhyar (1971) writes:

> The point is to be able to see where everything that happens at any time fits into the total pattern or structure of your existence.

> Those who look at life from the existential point of view, seeing all as an absurdity, are destroying the health and vitality of man, as Victor Frankel's experiments have shown. What man needs more than anything else to be healthy is a sense of meaning. Meaningfulness is defined as passing through a number of phases which, related one to the other, become the frame of reference for whatever happens in your life. *Showing man the meaningfulness of his life is the most important thing that astrology can do* . . .. (p. 4)

> Astrology is significant because it can demonstrate that life lends itself to a meaningful interpretation. (p. 5)

One reason for astrology's nefarious reputation in scientific and academic circles during the past decades is that most astrology (and almost all popular astrology) was still concerned with the prediction of definite events, rather than with the inner life of the individual person. The most important step that Rudhyar's Humanistic Astrology takes is that it shifts the emphasis from the outer world of events to the inner world of personal experience and growth. Various "predictive" techniques, such as progressions and transits, still have a place in a humanistically oriented astrology; but the significance of what such techniques indicate changes from a deterministic, meaningless act of destiny to a meaningful opportunity to experience and integrate new aspects of one's way of being. In other words, those times indicated as crucial (by the analysis of the cycles most vital to the person's individual pattern of growth) are seen as part of a larger pattern of growth and self-actualization. Hence, even difficult experiences assume a positive, growth-producing personal significance. Rudhyar (1971) explains this new emphasis on the individual person in astrology this way:

> If you want astrology to demonstrate its genius, you must focus on that which is unique to astrology, in which it has the capacity to give the fullest value. That is the individual situation.
>
> What you are trying to understand is the meaning of that situation as a whole. The reason the position of the planets is important is simply this: if you realize the universe is an organism in the broadest sense of the term, a system of integrated activities, then anything that happens within that system of integrated activity has a place and function within that system. If you want to understand a particular point in time-space within that system, you have to see it in relation to the whole system. The wholeness of the system is constantly working in polyphonic harmony with the life of the individual which has become separated from the whole by becoming itself, a little whole, a little organism. Each time anything individualizes out from the whole, it remains part of the whole.... The idea in astrology is to relate all the functional activity of a human being to ten basic symbols, or planets, each planet representing a definite quality of activity. Taken together, they represent a blueprint of a person as a whole. (p. 4)

In his booklet *Astrology for New Minds* (1969) Rudhyar explains this point:

> ... every individual person is a relatively independent organic whole in which a multitude of forces dynamically interact according to an original and originating pattern which establishes its life-purpose and its basic relation to all other wholes in the universe. This organic whole — the individual person — is essentially no different from the almost infinitely greater and vaster organized Whole, which we call the universe. Indeed the individual person constitutes one particular aspect of the universal Whole, *focused* at a particular point in space and in terms of the particular need for it at the exact moment of its emergence into independent existence. This is the moment of the first breath because it is then that the individual's basic rhythms of existence are established within a particular environment. (p. 27)

Since, as Rudhyar writes, the"*substantial* elements or basic drives in *every* organized existential system are the same," and since human beings on Earth are part of the same whole as the planets in our solar system, we have a basis upon which to build a cosmic language appropriate to man's actual way of being and pattern of functioning. In a lecture given at the American Federation of Astrologers Convention (1968), Rudhyar summed up what he considered to be astrology's most important use:

> Simply this: to live a more conscious, more understanding life in terms of a more objective realization of the character and relative meaning of the basic factors which structure your existence, and the existence of people around you.. . . . it is a way of wisdom.

Today, humanistic psychologists are attempting to create a psychology which emphasizes such positive factors as self-actualization, creativity, attaining higher consciousness, and realizing in an immediate way one's essential self. In astrology, the humanistically oriented psychologist, educator, counselor, or layman may find his most powerful and useful tool; for astrology presents us with a language which precisely describes the unique combination of universal factors operating within each of us.

7

The Uses of Astrology in the Counseling Arts

The previous chapters have already outlined some of the primary values and uses of astrological insights within the domain of psychology in general. Astrology is equally applicable to other areas of the counseling arts, whether they be marriage counseling, child and family counseling, specific types of psychotherapy, or merely the sort of counseling that many of us do in our everyday lives, whether or not we have the title of "psychologist." Since the most important theoretical considerations have already been dealt with quite thoroughly in previous chapters, in this chapter I simply want to point to some specific and practical applications of astrology in the whole area of counseling. As most readers probably know, there are many types of astrology, complete with their particular symbolic correlations appropriate for the subject at hand, and there are many applications of the basic astrological laws. But it is in the area of the counseling arts that I am particularly interested, and so I feel that sharing some of the insights I have gained using astrology everyday in a rather large counseling practice might be of some relevance to the reader's experience.

I especially want to emphasize that counseling is an *art* and that it is in the one-to-one counseling situation that astrology's symbols come alive most immediately. The art of counseling is an interchange of energy with another person, a way of elucidating the realities of the client's total life situation and individual way of being. Although one can improve one's abilities in the counseling situation by experience, devoted practice, and penetrating self-examination, the art itself cannot be taught. Since every individual is different, his or her particular way of utilizing astrology in counseling will differ from any other person's approach. I myself am not particularly interested in playing the "guru" or in structuring my professional practice in such a way that people come to me expecting me to do all the work, all the talking, and to deliver to them all the answers to their own individual dilemmas. It is clear to me that the openness of the client in each situation in fact determines how much help or what depth of increased self-knowledge he or she will gain from our interchange. This is true in every life situation: we program what we will receive by how much we are willing to give and how open we are to facing the truth about ourselves. The fact that some astrologers continue to play the role of fortune-teller or all-knowing channel for cosmic wisdom is merely an indication that such practitioners have their ego too wrapped up in that role. Astrologers, no matter how they see themselves or how the public may view them, are merely human beings like any others, with limited knowledge, limited understanding, and limited experience. They differ from other people only in that they have studied (hopefully with some depth) this system of cosmic symbols which provides them with a tool that can enable them to penetrate below the surface of ego, self-deception, and social roles.

In the everyday practice of astrology as a profession, it is of the utmost importance that the practitioner's intellectual honesty be uncompromising. In other words, if he doesn't know an answer to a question, doesn't understand some aspect of the birth-chart, or doesn't really have a rapport with the person at a certain level, he should not hesitate to say so and therefore to ask for help or clarification. I realize that most astrologers are often confronted with a client's desire to dump all responsibility in the astrologer's lap and to project the image of "guru" onto the astrologer. This is a game that the ego loves, and it is therefore easy to fall into such a role without realizing the real implications of doing so. However, one should realize that merely giving advice without also giving a means of deeper understanding is of little value, for each person must do his or her own work and must, through his or her own experience, arrive at the higher awareness that enables the person to outgrow or to transcend the difficulty. At the same time, the astrologer should realize the power at his disposal and the amazing sensitivity to suggestion that human beings have, and he should use that power with the utmost caution. It is better to say nothing than to make an unfounded guess based on insufficient understanding merely because of the ego's insecurity or because of the client's demands. As Zipporah Dobyns has pointed out, behind the astrologer's statements, as far as the client is able to perceive, lies the power and authority of the cosmos. This is a responsibility that should not be taken lightly. In addition, one's intellectual honesty should extend to the point where the counselor should freely state his own particular philosophical beliefs and ethics if they are interfering with his ability to deal objectively with a particular person or situation.

The relationship between the astrologer and client is as deeply personal as that between a doctor and patient. The quality of that relationship is inevitably a determining factor in the ultimate outcome of the consultation. Therefore, no astrologer should feel hesitant about referring a person to another astrologer if he or she feels that some tension or resistance in a particular relationship makes it impossible to deal effectively and openly with the client. There is no question of who is the "best" astrologer. There are simply different types of astrologers for different types of people. What one astrologer is not able to understand or to deal with may be precisely the greatest strength of another practitioner. It is not only the particular system of astrology or specific kinds of astrological techniques used, therefore, which determine the quality of astrological practice; it is more importantly the quality of relationship and the depth of self-knowledge which illuminate the one-to-one interchange. Without the benefit of the person-to-person interchange in astrological work, it is impossible to use astrological procedures in the deepest way and with the greatest possible benefits. Although doing a chart for someone one hasn't seen can indeed be helpful to the person, that individual would generally derive much deeper understanding from personal contact with the astrologer. For, without immediate personal contact, it is impossible to know (unless one is truly a gifted psychic) the level of awareness with which the individual will respond to his or her inner and outer circumstances.

In the remainder of this chapter, I will simply list some of the values that astrology can contribute to the counseling arts. These are my own personal values and are naturally associated with my particular experience and with my particular attitude toward life.

1. The Hindu holy book *Bhagavad Gita* states that the "mind is the slayer of the real." A modern author has written, "The death of ego is the birth of everything else." Utilizing astrology can provide a perspective upon and a detachment from our mind and ego patterns in order that we may again occasionally perceive what is real; for, as long as we are victimized by these patterns, we are in total darkness. The birth-chart reveals these patterns in a clear way that enables us to deal more effectively with our habits and with ourselves.

2. Astrology helps one to develop patience; for, when it is seen that the primary structural aspects of one's existence are subject to an already-established periodicity and cyclic rhythm, it is much easier to dwell in the present with a patient acceptance of the here and now and with the knowledge that the present phase will end when it has outlived its purpose. The kind of patience that can develop with the aid of astrology has been defined by one author as "an active alignment with the timing of God."

3. Astrology provides a pattern of growth and development that is far superior to any other psychological tool. It indicates what one should be working on, the essential meaning of a particular experience or phase of life, what inner patterns one is coming to terms with, the approximate duration of any particular phase of experience, and an accurate way of timing crucial changes in life.

4. Astrology enables one to tune in on his or her inner powers and to use the power of thought, will, and creative vitality to mold a better way of being. By paying attention to astrological cycles, we can see when we have the opportunity to develop new approaches to life and when we will be tested to see if our present approaches are truly fulfilling and creative.

5. Astrological study or familiarity with astrological practice through a counseling experience enables one to understand more deeply the Universal Laws that pervade all of life and help the individual to rely upon these universal truths in one's own inner life. Among these laws are: order, compensation (or balance), cause and effect (karma), vibration, cycles, polarity, "what ye think ye become," and "like begets like."

6. Astrology in the counseling arts reveals how any experience fits into the larger pattern of order that constitutes one's basic life structure or life plan.

7. Astrology gives us a sense of perspective and a means of gaining awareness on our lives, so that we don't get "hung up" on one experience, frustration, or blockage. It can get us in touch with the dynamism and cyclic nature of all life.

8. Astrology can provide us with faith in something greater than mere ego consciousness and therefore faith in one's *real* self.

9. Astrology helps the counselor or therapist to *get inside* the client, to attune to him according to the client's own nature rather than projecting his unconscious assumptions on the individual. It also enables him to choose appropriate treatment or therapy for a particular person.

10. Astrology can provide us with the key to the initiations (i.e., the crucial times of confrontation and marked growth) in every person's life, a pattern and need which is ignored by Western culture.

11. Astrology provides a means whereby the client's deepest feelings and unconscious yearnings may be brought to awareness and given form. What originally was a vague, troublesome annoyance can then be transformed into a reservoir of newly-liberated creative energy, often giving the individual a clear sense of new direction and meaning in life.

12. Astrology enables the person to determine the type of activity in which his or her life-energies can flow with the greatest amount of ease and satisfaction.

13. Astrology can help people to have a greater confidence in themselves by confirming the intimations, feelings, and inner knowledge that they may have been afraid to express or to trust. Rather than the often-voiced criticism of astrology that it makes one weaker by depending on forces outside the self, the proper use of astrology can help an individual to develop a greater degree of self-reliance and self-confidence. So often, a person feels deeply that he has special abilities in a certain area, for example, but the lack of confidence or trust in self may make it difficult to act upon this feeling.

14. Astrology can help us to know that "all the world is a stage" and that we are merely playing a part in this vast drama. Such a realization can give us a sense of perspective and humor that alone makes life easier to deal with. And, in addition, such a realization leads one eventually to consider the ultimate questions of life: Who is the actor in this drama? Who is the director? And who is the author?

15. Astrology shows us that within us are many interacting dynamics, that our being in the material world comprises many forces, needs, and urges. Astrology helps us to identify with the totality of this living process rather than identifying, as most people do, with one or two limited dimensions of experience.

16. The use of astrology in the counseling arts enables the counselor to help the person to align himself with the truth of his nature and being, rather than molding him to fit a man-made theory of how he should be.

8

Notes on Education & the Training of Astrological Counselors

Anyone involved in American education, either as a student, a teacher, an administrator, or a parent, is gradually coming to the realization that our educational institutions are archaic. Not only the structure of the curriculum but also the very assumptions upon which the entire system is based are due for a thorough transformation. Many parents nowadays are so disgusted with public school education that they are organizing their own "free" schools — often at the price of great financial hardship — in order that their children can learn and grow in a healthy atmosphere, free from overly-competitive and coercive measures. Some of these people have come to the conclusion that a school as such, divorced from the everyday life of a *community*, is itself outdated. And so we see in almost every state of the union the rapid growth of communities of people who share similar goals and values and who are beginning to integrate the education of their children into the whole structure of their life-styles.

What indeed is meant by the word "education"? Most people and even most dictionaries limit its meaning to the process of conveying information by instruction, training, and practice. The deepest meaning of the word, however, etymologically signifies "to lead out" or "to draw out." I think we can assume that this process refers to *leading one out of darkness* into the light, or *drawing out* the essence of what is already there within the individual. Hence we can see that education is really a much subtler process than what it is usually assumed to be. Its true purpose is not so much the memorization of data in order that the student can become a smoothly functioning human computer, but rather the abolition of fear and the guided growth of awareness. This is not to say that there is no place in modern education for the teaching of technical skills; but what I am emphasizing here is the fact that no amount of technical knowledge can outweigh the need for individual psychological and emotional growth. If our universities are to be merely vocational training schools (as most of them are becoming), then they should be recognized as such instead of maintaining the fallacy that their purposes are the pursuit of truth and the shaping of character.

I feel that one great problem in our educational system is that the schools are trying to be all things to all people. Grammar schools try to serve the purposes of babysitters, moral teachers, socialization agencies, and places where children learn basic communication and mathematical skills. Added to all these responsibilities is the attempt to provide special classes and guidance for those emotionally disturbed youngsters whose parents have failed them. High schools — no longer able to baby-sit teenagers — usually have the atmosphere of prisons; and, except for a special few who are achievement-oriented in academically-defined ways, the high schools provide little stimulation and immense frustration for their students. Universities and colleges, except for a few private schools, are trying to do so many things that the chaos we read about in newspapers is an inevitable result. They are trying to accomplish everything from vocational training and specialized professional work to minority education and large-scale social change. I feel that some semblance of order can be achieved in our society's educational programs if we are open-minded enough to take a few lessons from the most ancient pattern of order and individual development: astrology.

In the zodiac, four phases of individual education are symbolized. These are the mutable signs: Gemini, Virgo, Sagittarius, and Pisces. (Actually, if we consider "education" in its broadest ramifications, each zodiacal sign represents a phase of individual selfhood, growth, and hence personal "education." Ideally, all of these phases of growth, patterns of development, and ways of being should be taken into consideration by any teacher. But for the purposes of institutional and social ordering of the phases of marked *mental-spiritual growth*, the mutable signs are sufficient.) These four stages in individual education can be defined as follows:

GEMINI represents the level of primary social involvement and the attainment of basic intellectual skills. Included in this stage of development is the formation of the child's first peer-relationships, both within and without the family. This phase also symbolizes the child's first attempts to think his own thoughts, to look at the world in his own way, and to "figure out" (through rational processes) and express his perceptions. Hence, *communication,* the key word of the sign Gemini, here operates on both the social and intellectual level.

VIRGO represents the period of service to society, apprenticeship to a master of the craft with which the person will earn his livelihood, and initial contact with the everyday practical world of hard work, duties, and responsibilities. This phase of personal growth is almost entirely neglected in our culture. Hence, we have thousands — even millions — of college-educated young people who graduate and are appalled to realize that they can't really *do* anything. Their higher education has filled their heads with volumes of unapplied and often impractical ideas; and meanwhile, they have acquired no real *skill* with which to make a living in the world. Since many of them are now at least *amateur* scholars or intellectuals, it is difficult and frustrating for them to go backward from the ninth house phase of higher education to the sixth house phase of toil and servitude. A great improvement in our nation's educational program would result from the establishment of apprenticeship periods immediately following the end of the Gemini phase (at ages 14-16). If this ancient initiation into the everyday world were revived in our country, many young people would find themselves quite content with a work that they enjoyed. Then the Sagittarius phase could follow naturally.

SAGITTARIUS symbolizes the phase of development that grows naturally from the Virgo phase of apprenticeship. Sagittarius and the ninth house are often said to represent "higher education;" but in a broader sense, it symbolizes the attainment of *mastery* in one's chosen field, whether it manifests as a master craftsman or as a practitioner of one of the highly-vaunted "professions." This is the phase of individual education where one begins to have a marked effect upon the world at large, whether through teaching new apprentices, publishing the fruits of one's labors, or establishing standards for future generations. Hence, this phase of development includes both learning (in the sense of perfecting one's work and one's ideals and character) and dispensing what one has learned. In traditional education in the USA, we have mistakenly assumed that anyone with a Ph.D., M.D., or other higher degree is a master of his field. We have overlooked the fact that true mastery comes only after a period of rigid self-discipline, painstaking toil, and the gradual development of humility based on the realization that one could really know nothing without the labors of his predecessors. Just because we channel people as quickly as possible through all sorts of academic programs in order to "turn out" so many Ph.D.s or M.D.s does not mean that we have enriched our culture with that many true masters. We sacrifice quality for quantity simply to maintain the illusion that excellence can be had cheaply.

PISCES represents the phase of individual development that comes after one has completed his work in society, fulfilled his familial obligations, and has felt the compelling need to turn within himself in order to experience the most refined and essential type of education: the education of the spiritual man. In India, although the tradition is slowly changing, there exists a basic pattern of life closely related to the four stages we are describing. The last usually manifests in the person retiring from the world (including relatives) and devoting himself or herself to spiritual disciplines. This Pisces phase then symbolizes *devotion* and the sacrifice of one's worldly attachments in order to become a channel for the manifestation and realization of a greater truth, a more comprehensive whole. The great psychologist C.G. Jung wrote an essay called "The Stages of Life" in which he describes a normal pattern of conscious growth very similar to the one we are considering here. The last stage, according to Jung, is a marked turning inward toward spiritual realizations.

The Relationship of Teacher and Student

Astrology can also help us to deal with each other as distinct, individual persons, while at the same time realizing that we are all part of the same universe, merely different manifestations of the same *whole*. This very distinctness of individual persons is a factor relevant to education that is almost entirely neglected in teacher-training programs. The fact is that most teachers (most people, in fact) have never really accepted the truth that people are indeed different. Naturally, such an acceptance requires a certain degree of self-knowledge on the part of the teacher. Without this basic acceptance of others' differences, a teacher will unconsciously impose his or her own biases and expectations upon the pupils. Hence, a Cancer teacher (i.e., Cancer Sun sign) may absolutely detest a Libra child or be very threatened by an Aries. This would undoubtedly be detrimental to the student's progress in school. I have personally witnessed numerous examples of this prejudice in teacher-student relationships. It is a sad thing to watch, but it is even sadder to realize that a short course in astrology in our teacher-training programs is absolutely forbidden even though it would alleviate many such problems.

Since most teachers have no knowledge of astrology (which is in fact an accurate way of categorizing people and of gaining *perspective* on inter-personal relationships), they naturally fall back on other, less-accurate ways of categorizing and evaluating students. The chief means of student evaluation, although numerous studies have revealed the harmful effects of its use, remains the I.Q. Test. Students are thus categorized according to how well they are able to accomplish certain intellectual functions. The I.Q. Test erroneously claims to determine the "intelligence" of the students, but it overlooks the fact that there are different kinds of "intelligence." "Intelligence" is one of those words like "education;" it means whatever it is defined to mean for a particular purpose. In fact, although I.Q. tests were originally meant to measure "intelligence," they now are said by honest experts in the field of psychological testing to measure simply what I.Q. tests measure. That may sound absurd, and it is! But nevertheless, many teachers continue to rely on such tests to evaluate students. And the teacher's initial expectations of a student's performance are often based solely upon the numerical result of these tests!

A study of astrology will show the teacher that there are indeed different kinds of intelligence and talents. The only psychic function that most "educators" seem to be interested in is the intellect, symbolized astrologically by Mercury. Mercury's position and aspects can clearly reveal how well integrated and smoothly functioning the rational faculty is; but a consideration of Venus may reveal artistic talents, Mars mechanical or engineering abilities, Neptune musical sensitivity, etc. The fact is that different people excel at different things, and a study of astrology can give the teacher patience and a way of approaching and understanding different sorts of students. A highly-evolved child may be in tune with much higher levels of consciousness and imagination than is his teacher. Hence, the teacher above all needs to *recognize* his students' talents and attunements and needs to learn to let the child be free to grow *in his own way*. Astrology can help him to accomplish this.

Obviously, no teacher can be all things to all people; and any teacher will have his or her failings, biases, likes, and dislikes. The important thing about a teacher learning astrology, however, is that he can then get a perspective on his biases, and therefore deal with his students more objectively. I think the most important thing for the teacher to realize is his or her own fallibility. When the teacher is honest about his own feelings and mistakes, the student feels trust and personal respect for the teacher. The words of C.G. Jung express the crucial essence of the teacher's difficult job:

> For the day will inevitably come when what the educator teaches by word of mouth no longer works, but only what he is. Every educator — and I use the term in its widest sense — should constantly ask himself whether he is actually fulfilling his teachings in his own person and in his own life, to the best of his knowledge and with a clear conscience. Psychotherapy has taught us that in the final reckoning it is not knowledge, not technical skill, that has a curative effect, but the personality of the doctor. And it is the same with education: it presupposes self-education. ("The Significance of the Unconscious in Individual Education")

The Training of Astrological Counselors

Anyone who has been actively involved in the field of astrology during the past few years is well aware of the difficulty encountered whenever any individual or group attempts to set standards of education or training for astrological practitioners. The outcry inevitably heard soon thereafter is not totally a result of the individualistic personality characteristics of astrologers; it is also the result of the realization among many in the astrological field that their particular methods of practice are not readily included or defined by rules, regulations, and legal conveniences. The fact that there are almost as many different kinds of astrological practice as there are astrologers makes it difficult to design any training program, set of educational requirements, or piece of regulating legislation that would be fair to all and still be specific enough to serve a well-defined purpose. It is not my aim here to deal with the question of licensing astrological practitioners, nor do I want to give the impression that academic training in the traditional sense is an acceptable answer to the current need for specific structures or guidelines which can be helpful to astrological students and which can improve the quality of astrological practice for the general public. In the remainder of this chapter, I merely want to define some specific issues that should be taken into consideration by any individual or group that sets out to establish a channel whereby students or novice practitioners develop astrological counseling skills.

It is imperative to make a clear distinction between *astrology* and *astrological counseling*. Whereas *astrology* in itself is simply a body of knowledge like any other field of study, comprising traditions, a history, and certain established techniques and relationships, *astrological counseling* is the application of this body of knowledge for the purpose of helping people in a practical way to become more aware of themselves, their life-structures, creative potentials, and relationships. Whereas *astrology* can be taught, researched, and tested in ways that are compatible with the usual academic procedures in other fields, *astrological counseling* is a highly individualized art which cannot be "taught" past a certain point and which cannot be regulated or tested in rigidly-dogmatic ways. Those active in the field of astrology primarily as researchers, computer programmers, statisticians, and technicians need not have the skills of a counselor or therapist in order to perform their work well. But those who seek to apply astrological knowledge to a specific human situation not only should be familiar with the basic science of astrology, but also need to concern themselves with the psychological realm of experience, the quality of their capacity for personal relationship, and the ethical questions which inevitably arise in any extended person-to-person work.

An excellent article entitled "The Teaching of Astrology" appeared in the Summer, 1975 issue of the Journal of the British Astrological Association. The author, David Hamblin, M.A., a university teacher, focuses with great depth and insight on the entire question of how astrology is taught today and what the ideal preparation would be for astrological researchers and counselors. In the article, Hamblin makes a distinction between "astrology" and "astrotherapy" similar to that mentioned in the last paragraph; and he notes that "in existing courses the two are mixed up, so that neither is taught properly." He points out that most courses in astrology nowadays are based on the assumption that the completion of the course will enable the student to be a skilled "astrotherapist," a fallacy analagous to the assumption that pasing a driving test for a license means that the individual is an accomplished and skilled driver. He is usually, in fact, only beginning to develop the skills which experience alone can teach. Mr. Hamblin therefore suggests that the ideal course in astrology would consist of two distinct parts. Part I would deal only with "pure" astrology and would alone be sufficient training for researchers, statistical experimenters, etc. This course would include not only instruction in the traditional astrological factors and interpretive meanings, but would also give the student a working familiarity with the many modern innovations in the field, even those which are not yet fully developed or widely-utilized: harmonics, midpoints, solar arc progressions, solar returns, the vertex, key cycles, fixed stars, and planetary pictures. Also included in this course would be the historical development of astrology, astrology's relationship to other fields of study, a thorough familiarity with the acknowledged pioneers in astrology (Rudhyar, Carter, Jones, etc.), and an in-depth study of the better insights and methods of modern psychology.

Part II of the course would be what Hamblin calls "astrotherapy." He writes: "It should be an essentially practical course, and its purpose should be, not just to help the student to interpret birth charts, but to help him to establish satisfactory relationships with his clients." Included in this part of his model course would be: an arrangement through which the student himself would be "astro-analyzed" by a tutor; practice sessions working with clients under the guidance of the tutor, which afterwards would be discussed and evaluated; and group sessions in which students would comment on each other's interpretations *and* interviewing skills. Hamblin admits that such a course of study, including both parts, would take much longer and would be much more expensive than most existing courses, but he feels that this would be desirable since the end result would be that a "graduate" of such a program would be much more qualified and have far broader knowledge and experience than many currently-practicing astrologers. As he writes:

> At present it is almost as cheap to take the Diploma (British Faculty of Astrological Studies) course as it is to obtain a full analysis from a top-grade astrologer. We would think it ridiculous if it was as cheap to become a doctor as it is to consult a doctor; but, for some reason, the same situation seems less ridiculous in astrology.

I have quoted Hamblin's article at such length because I feel that he has very clearly defined some important problems in the area of astrological education. Although most astrologers nowadays are primarily self-taught and although I don't see this as necessarily a detriment, it is a fact that a rapidly-growing segment of the population in the United States is participating in a wide variety of educational programs related to astrology; and therefore it is becoming increasingly necessary to design programs that are specifically oriented toward people who are becoming astrological counselors, whether or not they classify themselves that way, and whether or not they will become full-time professionals in the field.

My own feeling is that, although the training of astrological counselors cannot be and should not be too rigidly controlled or necessarily incorporated into traditional academic structures complete with degrees, irrelevant requirements for admission, and an overly-authoritarian framework, the opportunity for such training in some form should be readily available for all serious students. Although astrological counseling cannot be "taught" in the traditional sense, acquiring such skills can be guided, and the student can benefit from the support of those who have the experience, insight, and capacity for honest relationship which the student can respect. There is no substitute in any person-to-person art for the daily lessons which diligent practice will bring to awareness; but there is likewise no substitute for the insight that can be gained from even brief contact with someone whose experience and understanding surpass one's own. The main purpose of any program in astrological counseling should be in accord with the true meaning of the word "education": *drawing out* the essence of the student's individual uniqueness, experience, inner knowledge, and psychic sensitivity; and guiding the growth of awareness by *leading out* the student from the darkness of ego-games, self-doubt, and self-consciousness. Through the encouragement and support of peers and "teachers," the participant in such a program could grow in self-knowledge through uncompromising self-examination and through an increasing attunement to a guiding ideal. Needless to say, this level of self-knowledge would be positively reflected in the individual's work as an astrological counselor.

It may be apparent to the reader that the kind of practical training program outlined above correlates with the Virgo phase of education described at the beginning of this chapter. This phase of development is missing almost completely from the educational patterns in our culture, including the usual mode of astrological education. Many astrologers learn the basics (Gemini) and leap right into teaching and writing (Sagittarius) without going through the refining process of apprenticeship and lengthy practical experience (Virgo). This results in a noticeable gap in the real knowledge of many astrological teachers and writers, for often they are merely repeating what they learned from someone else and have neither tested it in practice nor augmented it with new insights. Gemini and Sagittarius, when not supported by practical experience (Virgo), tend to be shallow and totally speculative. A teacher or writer in the astrological field should ideally have a deep reservoir of experience from which to draw, rather than just a multitude of ideas and ideals that have never been tested through practical application. It is my hope that all astrologers and students of astrology will come to accept this need for intellectual honesty and for diligent work at this Virgo phase of development, whether through an established program or simply through self-disciplined and patient individual practice. The Virgo virtue of humility is a valuable end-product of such effort, for we inevitably find how little we really know, no matter what the extent of our experience may be. And this humility makes us better instructors and more understanding and open-minded counselors for others.

Part II

The Four Elements:

An Energy Approach to
Interpreting Birth-Charts

9

Astrology: A Language of Energy

Although astrology has been described in terms of symbolism, karma, synchronicity, psychological functions, planetary "rays," and so on, most astrologers have overlooked the basic foundation upon which astrology is based: *energy*. Indeed, all physical and mental life is a manifestation of energy. When the great astrologer Dane Rudhyar wrote "Planets in a chart represent modes of functional activities within an organized whole," he was referring to specific energies that operate in each of us. Probably, the reason we have overlooked the *energy* foundation of all astrological phenomena is the fact that it is too obvious. It sometimes seems easier to develop elaborate schemes and theories rather than to open our eyes to what's right in front of us.

In the field of modern psychology and parapsychology, researchers are now beginning to emphasize the importance of energy flow and energy blocks in dealing with their clients. Psychotherapeutic techniques such as Gestalt Therapy, Structural Integration, and Bio-Energetics are more and more concentrating on mobilizing the client's own energies and integrating these energies into a functional whole. Likewise, this is the purpose of astrology when applied to psychological and physical problems.

Researchers in Bio-Energetic Therapy, which has developed from the works of Wilhelm Reich, are now measuring and even *seeing* the energy fields that emanate from living organisms. Dr. Robert O. Becker, an orthopedic surgeon at New York's Upstate Medical Center, has achieved remarkable results from his research correlating the body's magnetic field with biological cycles and changes in the earth's geomagnetic field. Dr. Becker has even traced negative electrical currents emitted from broken bones and changes in the electrical charge of the brain and nervous system, all of which promise a science of healing based upon energy for the future. (See Appendix A for more information on Dr. Becker's work.)

An osteopath and chiropractor named Dr. Randolph Stone, whom we will mention again later, has already developed an energy approach to healing, called "Polarity Therapy," that harmonizes with astrological principles. Dr. Stone has written many books on the subject, among which are *Energy: The Vital Principle in the Healing Art* and *The Wireless Anatomy of Man.* Astrologers have long known that the natal horoscope can be used for diagnosis of physical ailments, but Dr. Stone's work provides a definite technique for changing the blocked energy fields and currents. (For a full explanation of Polarity Therapy, see Appendix C.)

Other popular books which have dealt with the question of energy in the healing arts are *Psychic Discoveries Behind the Iron Curtain,* Dr. Karagulla's *Breakthrough to Creativity,* and Ruth Montgomery's *Born to Heal.* All of this modern research into the importance of energy in both healing and astrology is really nothing new. Clairvoyants such as Eileen Garrett and Edgar Cayce have long claimed to see "auras" surrounding each person from which they are able to diagnose and even predict illness or psychological crises. (See Appendix B for more on Eileen Garrett's work.) However, there is one thing missing in all these attempts to describe people's energy, and that is a proper language. Those engaged in the healing arts, whether psychological or physical, need a language in order to differentiate accurately between all the various energies operating in the human organism. Astrology can provide us with that language; in fact, astrology could be to the healing arts what the periodic table is to chemistry: the foundation for a new healing science.

The reason the natal horoscope is drawn for the exact moment of the first breath is that it is only then that the newborn human organism begins to exchange energy with the universe *in an immediate way,* uninfluenced by the energies of the mother. At the moment of the first breath, the infant begins his own rhythm of life; he establishes his own individual attunement with the energies of the universe. Astrology indicates that certain specific energies and energy patterns are established at birth and continue to operate within and through an individual person during the course of his entire life. If anything in astrology can be said to be "fated" or predetermined, it is this initial attunement to the energies of the cosmos that takes place at birth. But what any individual will do with these energies and how he will direct them can only be determined within the limits of the astrologer's experience and subtlety of perception.

The Zodiacal Signs as Energy Patterns

The four elements of astrology (fire, earth, air, and water) are the basic building blocks of all material structures and organic wholes. Each element represents a basic kind of energy and consciousness that operates within each of us. Just as modern physics has shown that energy *is* matter, these four elements interweave and combine to form all matter. When the spark of life leaves a human body at death, the four elements all dissociate and return to their primal state. It is only life itself, manifesting in an organized, living whole, that holds together the four elements. All four are in every person, although each person is consciously more attuned to some types of energy than others. Each of the four elements manifests in three vibrational modalities: cardinal, fixed, and mutable. Hence, when we combine the four elements with the three modalities, we have twelve primary patterns of energy which are called the zodiacal signs.

The zodiacal signs have also been called "energy fields," archetypal patterns, universal formative principles, etc. (See Chapter 4.) These are all names for the same reality. These universal formative principles are the living realities which astrology symbolizes, and they are identical with Jung's "archetypes." What Jung says about the archetype can also be applied to the fundamental nature of the zodiacal energy patterns: ". . . it seems to me probable that the real nature of the archetype is not capable of being made conscious, that it is transcendent." If indeed the true nature of the energy patterns represented by the zodiacal signs is transcendent and unknowable, the most I can do to give a hint of the sort of energy patterns mentioned here is to tell you to look at your own hand. The same energies which built the unique patterns seen in the palm and on the fingertips continue to vitalize and to sustain not only the body, but also the psyche. One might ask: What indeed is the "psyche"? It can't be seen; yet it *is*. We experience the impact of psychic forces day in and day out. The psyche is, therefore, as real as any material object even though we cannot see or touch or smell or taste it.

If we can accept the reality of psychic forces, we can surely accept the reality of the unseen builders of all life, material and psychic. These unseen builders are the primal energy patterns or formative principles of the universe. Jung calls them the archetypes because they have been active in molding all life on this planet since the beginning of time. Astrologers call them the zodiacal signs and are mainly concerned with them in relation to the way they manifest in human beings as personality types. All of the keywords, qualities, and endless lists of characteristics commonly found in astrological textbooks grow from these essential roots: the twelve primary energy patterns commonly called the signs of the zodiac. An understanding of what is meant by these primary energy patterns is necessary for an in-depth approach to any kind of astrology, but in the case of Medical and Psychological Astrology, it is especially important that this essential, archetypal meaning be discovered and coherently formulated.

One way of understanding the various energy patterns represented by the zodiacal signs is to analyze them in terms of their modalities. The cardinal signs represent centrifugal radiating energy and correlate with the principle of *action in a definite direction*. The "positive" cardinal signs, Aries and Libra, are concerned with action in the present, based upon future considerations. The "negative" cardinal signs, Cancer and Capricorn, are more concerned with the past. (Witness, for example, Cancer's love of the home and antiques and Capricorn's concern with tradition and history.)

The fixed signs represent centripetal energy; that is, energy radiating inward toward a center. These signs are associated with the principle of inertia in their mundane manifestations, but they are also known for great powers of concentration and perseverance when the energy is used for creative activity or spiritual development. Of the three quadruplicities, the fixed signs are most centered in the here and now. The connection of the fixed signs with esoteric doctrines of rebirth and spiritual development arises from the great concentration of energy in these signs, which energy is radiating constantly within the person and is at least to some extent under his control. Hence, people born with the Sun in a fixed sign intuitively sense the depth and power of the life-giving spirit within them; and so these signs have been known as the "gates of the avatar" and as the key symbols of the major initiations of the soul because the concentrated energy also brings these people the potential for concentrated consciousness.

The mutable signs are correlated with the principle of harmony and may be conceived as spiralic patterns of energy. Pisces and Virgo symbolize spirals of energy directed downward; thus, these signs are connected with the past in some way: Pisces with past "karma" and Virgo with the past crises in the development of the personality. Gemini and Sagittarius symbolize spirals of energy directed upward; and these signs are future-oriented, giving rise to the prophetic tendencies of Sagittarians and the endless speculations of Gemini.

The element of any particular sign shows the specific type of consciousness and method of most immediate perception to which the individual is attuned. Air signs are correlated with the mind's sensation, perception, and expression, especially related to geometrical thought forms. Fire signs express the warming, radiating, energizing life principle which can manifest as enthusiasm and love or as ego. Water signs symbolize the cooling, healing, soothing principle of sensitivity and feeling response. Earth signs reveal an attunement with the world of physical forms and a practical ability to utilize the material world. The nature and function of these elements will be described in great detail in later chapters.

The zodiac was considered by the ancients to be the "Soul of Nature." If we see the zodiacal signs as the primary, archetypal energy patterns of the universe, we can then understand why the ancients gave such prominence to them. Conceiving of the zodiac in this way also finds support in the psychic readings of the clair-voyant Edgar Cayce, who stated, "Life is sustained in this cycle of vibration" (reading #900-448). Could the zodiac be referred to as a cycle of vibration? I think so. Cayce also mentions, "Every individual entity is on certain vibrations" (#1861-12). All of this should explain what we call the zodiacal signs. Now what about the planets?

The Planets as Energy Regulators

Man has long been conceived of as a microcosm of the entire universe. Ancient yoga speaks of the *chakras* (or energy centers) within each person; and many esoteric schools of thought have correlated various *chakras* with certain planets. This is so because the planets are related to us by the same vibratory energy waves which are latent within us and to which we respond. These *chakras*, therefore, are the centers within us which correspond to certain centers of energy in the solar system. The sign that a particular planet is in reveals the attunement of that energy wave or force within us. The planets generally symbolize basic forces or active centers in our solar system which manifest as fundamental psychological functions, urges, needs, and motivators. The planets in the signs serve, as it were, as primary stimuli in the energy fields of the signs. *They symbolize the universal principles which regulate all energy functions in any organic whole.* Another way of expressing this is to say that the planets characterize the mode of energy exchange between the individual human being and the universal storehouse. They represent the major active principles which form character and motivate all types of self-expression simultaneously on every level: mental, emotional, and physical.

In ancient terms, the planets symbolize the gods which must be worshipped. This means that these fundamental life forces cannot be ignored except at the peril of the individual. They must be recognized, paid due attention, and accepted; then the energy inherent in them can be consciously directed. If we are not aware of these forces in our lives, then we are at the mercy of them. The great sin for the Greeks was *hybris*, which indicated that an individual had the audacity and foolish pride to ignore the gods in some way. Naturally, the gods' *nemesis* (i.e., explosion of pent-up forces that were refused a proper channel) followed inevitably.

The Astrological Theory of Personality

In psychological astrology, the planets may be divided into three groups. The first group consists of the basic *personal* factors: Sun, Moon, Mercury, Venus, and Mars. These planets show what forces we can consciously direct or modify to some extent. These planets characterize the more obvious personality traits and strongest urges in the individual. Everyone experiences a sense of individuality and self-identity (Sun), a way of reacting spontaneously based on conditioned responses (Moon), an ability to reason and to exchange thoughts with others (Mercury), a need and capacity for love and close relationship (Venus), and a drive toward action, self-assertion, and sexual experience (Mars).

Underlying these basic personal factors are the deeper *motivational* and *collective* factors symbolized by Jupiter and Saturn. Although these two planets can be said to represent specific urges, they also indicate deep states of being experienced as superconscious (Jupiter) or subconscious (Saturn) needs. Their collective significance refers to their impact on how one wants to participate in the world at large and in relation to social activities. These planets represent the deeper currents of stability, tradition, and safety (Saturn) and future aspirations, sense of adventure, risk-taking, and personal growth (Jupiter).

The third group is comprised of Uranus, Neptune, and Pluto. This group symbolizes the most profound sources of change in life, transcendent dimensions of experience, and the most subtle energies to which we are attuned. These forces affect our more conscious faculties through inspiration, flashes of insight, intuition, innate knowledge not learned through the intellect, an urge to merge oneself in a greater whole, and a strong impulse toward refining one's deepest nature. When these energies come into play, the old patterns of life are shaken up and quickly change. All together, these three planets could be said to refer to *transpersonal* factors and to the *transformative* energies within the life of each of us.

Considered as the components of one whole energy system, these three groups of planets provide the practitioner with a complete and comprehensive theory of human personality and psychological functioning, a frame of reference founded upon both the need for security, love, and creativity, and the constant surges toward self-actualization, change, growth, and transcendence. When we approach the individual and life in general at the same level where life's essential energies operate, we can begin to see the mind and body as mutually-interacting, living energy fields rather than as rigid mechanistic devices. Such an understanding of the whole man can open the door to the development of a new kind of astrology, a science which is based upon the laws of life.

Key Concepts and Definitions

A key to the understanding of all astrology is within the reach of anyone who truly understands the meaning of the following definitions:

The **PLANETS** indicate specific *dimensions of experience*.

The **SIGNS** indicate specific *qualities of experience*.

The **HOUSES** indicate specific *fields of experience* wherein the energies of the planets and signs operate.

The **ASPECTS** (or angular relationships between the planets) reveal how various dimensions of experience are integrated within the individual.

These four factors comprise the astrological alphabet, and it is the art of combining the letters of this alphabet that results in the language of energy called astrology.

These factors are combined in the following way: A particular dimension of experience (indicated by a certain planet) will invariably be colored by the quality of the sign wherein it is placed in the individual's chart. This combination results in a specific urge toward self-expression and a particular need for fulfillment being defined. The individual will confront that dimension of life most immediately in the field of experience indicated by the planet's house position. And, although the urge to express or to fulfill that dimension of experience will be present in anyone having a certain planet-sign combination, the specific aspects to that planet reveal how easily and harmoniously the person can express that urge or fulfill that need.

Presented on the next few pages are some of the key concepts related to each sign and planet. The chapter on the "Elements and the Houses" explains the key concepts of the houses. (See Chapter 16.)

Key Concepts for the Planets

	Principle	Urges Represented	Needs Symbolized
SUN:	Vitality; sense of individuality; creative energy, radiant inner self (attunement of soul); *essential* values	Urge to be and to create	Need to be recognized and to express self
MOON:	Reaction; sub-conscious predisposition; feeling about self (self-image); conditioned responses	Urge to feel inner support; domestic and emotional security urge	Need for emotional tranquility and sense of belonging; need to feel right about self
MERCURY:	Communication; conscious mind (i.e., logical or rational mind)	Urge to express one's perceptions and intelligence through skill or speech	Need to establish connections with others; need to learn
VENUS:	Emotionally-colored tastes; values; exchange of energy with others through giving of self and receiving from others; sharing	Social and love urge; urge to express affections; urge for pleasure	Need to feel close to another; need to feel comfort and harmony; need to give of self's emotions
MARS:	Desire; will toward action; initiative; physical energy; drive	Self-assertive and aggressive urge; sex urge; urge to act decisively	Need to achieve desires; need for physical and sexual excitement
JUPITER:	Expansion; grace	Urge toward a larger order or to connect self with something greater than self	Need for faith, trust, and confidence in life and self; need to improve self

	Principle	Urges Represented	Needs Symbolized
SATURN:	Contraction; effort	Urge to defend self's structure and integrity; urge toward safety and security through tangible achievement	Need for social approval; need to rely on one's own resources and work
URANUS:	Individualistic freedom; freedom *of* ego-self	Urge toward differentiation, originality, and independence from tradition	Need for change, excitement and expression without restraint
NEPTUNE:	Transcendent freedom; unification; freedom *from* ego-self	Urge to escape from the limitations of one's self and of the material world	Need to experience a oneness with life, a complete merger with the whole
PLUTO:	Transformation; transmutation; elimination	Urge toward total rebirth; urge to penetrate to the core of experience	Need to refine self; need to let go of the old through pain

Positive-Negative Expression
of Planetary Principles

Each planetary principle can be expressed positively and creatively or negatively and self-destructively. In other words, one's
attunement to each dimension of experience may be in harmony
with higher law or in a state of disharmony and discord. This
results in the creative use or in the misuse of these various energies, forces, and attunements. The aspects to each planet must be
analyzed in order to understand the degree of harmony or discord
present within the individual.

	Positive Expression	*Negative Expression*
SUN:	Radiation of spirit; creative and loving pouring forth of self	Pride; arrogance; excessive desire to be special
MOON:	Responsiveness; inner contentment; flowing, adaptable sense of self	Oversensitivity; insecurity; inaccurate, inhibiting sense of self
MERCURY:	Creative use of skill or intelligence; reason and power of discrimination used to serve higher ideals; ability to come to agreement through objective understanding and clear verbal expression	Misuse of skill or intelligence; amorality through rationalization of anything; opinionated and one-sided "communication"
VENUS:	Love; give and take with others; sharing; generosity of spirit	Self-indulgence; greed; emotional demands; inhibition of affections

	Positive Expression	*Negative Expression*
MARS:	Courage; initiative; will-power consciously directed toward legitimate aim	Impatience; willfulness; violence; improper use of force or threats
JUPITER:	Faith; reliance on higher power or greater plan; open-ness to grace; optimism; openness to self's need for improvement	Over-confidence; laziness; scattering energy; leaving the work to others; irre-sponsibility; over-extending self or promising too much
SATURN:	Disciplined effort; accept-ance of duties and responsi-bilities; patience; organization; reliability	Self-restriction through too much reliance on self and lack of faith; rigidity; coldness; defensivenes; crippling inhibition, fearfulness, and negativity
URANUS:	Attunement to truth; originality; inventiveness; directed experimentation; respect for freedom	Willfulness; restless impatience; constant need for excitement and purpose-less change; rebellion; extremism
NEPTUNE:	Attunement with the whole; realization of spiritual dimension of experience; all-encompassing compassion; living an ideal	Self-destructive escapism; evasion of responsibilities and self's deepest needs; refusal to face one's motives and to commit self to anything
PLUTO:	Acceptance of the need to focus one's mind and will power on one's own transformation; having the courage to face one's deepest desires and com-pulsions and to transmute them through effort and intensity of experience	Compulsive expression of subconscious cravings; will-ful manipulation of others to serve one's own ends; ruthlessly using any means to avoid the pain of facing one's self; infatuation with power

The Elements of the Zodiacal Signs & Their Key Concepts

	KEY CONCEPT	A planet in this sign will be colored by these qualities
FIRE SIGNS		
CARDINAL: ARIES	Single-pointed release of energy toward *new* experience	Self-willed urge for action, self-assertion
FIXED: LEO	Sustained warmth of loyalty and radiant vitalization	Pride and urge for recognition, sense of drama
MUTABLE: SAGITTARIUS	Restless aspiration propelling one toward an ideal	Beliefs, generalizations, ideals
EARTH SIGNS		
CARDINAL: CAPRICORN	Impersonal determination to get things done	Self-control, caution, reserve and ambition
FIXED: TAURUS	Depth of appreciation related to immediate physical sensations	Possessiveness, retentiveness, steadiness
MUTABLE: VIRGO	Spontaneous helpfulness, humility, & need to serve	Perfectionism, analysis, fine discrimination

AIR SIGNS

CARDINAL: LIBRA	Harmonization of all polarities for self-completion	Balance, impartiality, tact
FIXED: AQUARIUS	Detached coordination of all people and concepts	Individualistic freedom, extremism
MUTABLE: GEMINI	Immediate perception and verbalization of all connections	Changeable curiosity, talkativeness, friendliness

WATER SIGNS

CARDINAL: CANCER	Instinctive nurturing and protective empathy	Feeling, reserve, moods, sensitivity, self-protection
FIXED: SCORPIO	Penetration through intense emotional power	Compulsive desires, depth, controlled passion, secrecy
MUTABLE: PISCES	Healing compassion for all that suffers	Soul-yearnings, idealism, oneness, inspiration, vulnerability

Functions of the Planets in the Signs

The sign position of this planet shows:

Basic *Personal* Factors:
Consciously-directed
action

SUN: how one *is* (the tone of being) and how one perceives life

MOON: how one *reacts* based on subconscious predisposition

MERCURY: how one *communicates and thinks*

VENUS: how one *expresses affection, feels appreciated, and gives of self*

MARS: how one *asserts self and expresses desires*

Collective Factors:
States of being

JUPITER: how one *seeks to grow and to experience trust in life*

SATURN: how one *seeks to establish and preserve self through effort*

Transpersonal Factors:
Transformative energies

The sign positions of **URANUS, NEPTUNE,** and **PLUTO** are indications of generational attitudes, but in the individual chart they are of much less importance than the house position and aspects of these planets. The aspects of these trans-saturnian planets to the personal planets reveal how one is attuned to the forces of change within his generation and how one is attuned to the forces of change within himself.

In terms of Jungian psychology, the trans-saturnian planets represent the functional modes of the Collective Unconscious, whereas the Moon and Saturn represent the structural patterns and subconscious needs of the Personal Unconscious. The Moon symbolizes the intangible, emotional security needs associated with the mother (inner support) and Saturn symbolizes the tangible, material security needs associated with the father (outer support).

10

The Four Elements: The Basic Energies of Astrology

In an effort to modernize astrology along the lines of material science, many astrological writers have disregarded or almost completely ignored the ancient concept of the four elements. Some writers state things like, "Now that science has given us the periodic table of chemistry, we know that there are many more than four elements." Other writers and teachers who still use the elements to some extent do not sufficiently explain what these "elements" are or how they function, nor do they seem to realize that the elements are indeed the very foundation of the zodiac and therefore of all astrology.

One of the best expositions on the four elements that I have been able to find is in the introduction to C.E.O. Carter's *An Encyclopedia of Psychological Astrology*, which I will refer to later in detail. After describing what he calls the "root-principles" of astrology, Carter states that the elements "are capable of being described from many standpoints and in great detail, but it is necessarily far from easy to understand, explain, and exemplify what are, in fact, no less than the basic laws of our solar system, if not of the universe." Carter further writes that astrology is a certain means of gaining some understanding of how these life principles operate, although "to comprehend them fully would require an intellectual grasp such as we may ascribe to the Architect of that System alone."

I agree completely with Carter that the four elements are not merely "symbols" or abstract concepts, but rather that they refer to the vital forces that make up the entire creation that can be perceived by the physical senses. (This is why the zodiac was referred to in ancient times as the "soul of nature.") The elements are therefore not only the foundation of astrology and all occult sciences, but they comprise everything we can normally perceive and experience. It is true that the elements, if taken as purely material factors, symbolize the four states of matter described in modern physics: earth is solid; water liquid; air gaseous; and fire plasma or radiant ionized energy. They may also be said to represent the four primary needs of any advanced organism: air, water, earth (or food), and fire (warmth). But this alone does not begin to reveal the true meaning of the elements.

As Manley P. Hall writes in his booklet *Unseen Forces*, "The four elements are the basis of, as well as the life behind, the four physical material elements — earth, fire, air, and water." He goes on to state that "All things superior to those four essences can be cognized only by spiritual vision." In other words, the four elements with which astrology deals transcend mere material chemistry. As Dr. William Davidson, M.D. states in his *Medical Astrology Lectures*, "behind chemistry is force." In our attempt to understand the real meaning of the elements, we should be careful not to confuse the outer results of these vital forces with the ultimate energizing factors.

Although at first glance it may seem a rather daring generalization to assert that the four elements have such a complete and encompassing scope of action, it will become apparent during the course of this work that evidence from many diverse cultures and fields of knowledge point to this fact. In the field of astrology alone, why is it that astrological factors have been used successfully to understand the nature of cycles, events, personal experiences, and changes in mundane affairs at every level: physical, social, economic, psychological, emotional, political, and so forth? Astrology would obviously not be so useful in such a wide variety of life activities if it did not indeed provide us with a language of life's essential dynamic forces. To understand what we are really working with in the practice of astrology, we must approach astrology itself on the level where it operates; and that is the level of energy patterns, energy flow, and energy transmutation. In order to grasp the essence of astrological science, one has to fully understand the elements; and, in order to do that, one needs to look at not only the physical and psychological significance of the elements, but also to view the elements from the vantage point of a high state of spiritual awareness.

World-wide Recognition of
the Four Elements

Many cultures throughout the world include the four elements in their philosophical, religious, or mythological traditions. Most of these traditions postulate one primary energy which then manifests as "stepped down" energy currents known as the elements, a process resembling the working of an electric transformer. This primary energy has been called by many names: prana, vital force, Qi, and others. The essential characteristics of this energy have been identical for all cultures, although the names given to the primary force and to the elements themselves have varied.

In Tibet, huge structures called "stupas" were built as gigantic symbols of the structure of creation. The base of the stupa was a large cube (representing earth), upon which rested a sphere (water), and on top of the sphere was a spiral-like structure (fire). Then at the very top was a half-moon (air) in which rested a small sphere ("ether", the Tibetans' word for the primary force from which the others flow). The stupa represented the foundation of Tibetan cosmology, and the elements were considered therefore to be the fundamental energies of the cosmos.

A similar conception of the elements is found in the holy scriptures of India (such as the *Bhagavad Gita*) and also in the philosophical basis of Indian Ayurvedic Medicine. Chinese philosophy and Acupuncture are founded on the concept of the elements. Like Tibetan and Indian expressions of their nature, the Chinese speak of five elements: "The five elements: wood, fire, earth, metal, water, encompass all the phenomena of nature. It is a symbolism that applies itself equally to man." (Su Wen) These five elements correlate with the four elements commonly used in the western world, with the addition of ether. Western tradition doesn't usually mention the fifth element since it is really distinct from the others and, in fact, the source of the other four.

Ancient Greek philosophy was also based on the doctrine of the elements, which were equated with man's four faculties: moral (fire), aesthetic and soul (water), intellectual (air), and physical (earth). Medieval and Renaissance Europe imported the idea of the elements chiefly from the writings of Galen and correlated them with four "humours" which in turn gave rise to four specific human temperaments. These are found in all of the early medical writings of Europe as well as in the works of Shakespeare and other literary artists. In Japan, we find many examples of the importance given to the elements. For example, in a Zen Buddhist tract on Bodhidharma written in the year 1004 A.D., our traditional four elements are represented as the four qualities that make up creation: light (fire), airiness, fluidity, and solidity.

The elements are also intricately woven into the fabric of mythology. In ancient Sumer, where religion encompassed every aspect and activity of life, the most important deities corresponded to the elements: Anu the heavens (air); Enlil the storm (fire); Ninhursaga the earth; and Enki the waters. The foregoing examples reveal how the elements themselves, like the zodiac, were considered not only a vital reality which had to be dealt with by ancient peoples, but indeed the foundation of reality itself.

Modern Descriptions

For most of us, lacking the highest spiritual vision, the closest we can come to an immediate apprehension and appreciation of the elements is to experience their workings in the healing arts. This approach to the elements will be dealt with in more detail later, but it would be useful here to mention how some modern writers view the elements. Dr. Randolph Stone, the originator of a system of healing called Polarity Therapy which is based on the theory of balancing the elements, calls the elements "the unseen builders of life's structures." He says that the elements are the "gears of life" which must mesh in harmony for there to be health of mind and body. He states in his writings that the elements are like plates in a battery through which life energy (or "prana") flows to energize them. Dr. Stone calls the elements "finer energy fields" whose workings bring about states of well-being or disease of mind or body.

Dr. Stone, who is at this writing 85 years old and retired from practice, holds degrees in osteopathy, chiropractic, and naturopathy. He states, however, that his insights into the workings of the elements came not from any orthodox training in the healing arts but rather from personal insight, over sixty years of experience with diverse and challenging cases, and — most of all — from personal instruction from various spiritual teachers and Indian physicians. It is remarkable that insights closely parallelling those of Dr. Stone are also expressed by a man who has had no contact with any of Dr. Stone's sources. "Mr. A.," by which name he is called in his biography by Ruth Montgomery entitled *Born to Heal*, had no education beyond grammar school and received instruction about the elements through his psychic senses. His understanding of the workings of life's finer forces enabled Mr. A. to be a channel for thousands of remarkable recoveries from seemingly incurable ailments.

Mr. A's description sounds considerably like Dr. Stone's reference to the elements as being like plates in a battery:

"This world we live in is composed of gases and energy. All substance — plant, animal, and human life — results from the unlimited combination of energy frequencies acting on these gases. Every plant, animal, and human has its own individual energy frequency to establish and maintain life, growth, and development. At birth, the first breath of life is our direct supply, our lifeline with the Universal Power. . . . So long as this energy is established and flows without obstruction, we are in tune with the Universal supply of energy."

The astrological birth-chart is of course drawn for the moment of first breath, that instant when we immediately establish our lifelong attunement with the cosmic energy sources. The birth-chart therefore reveals your energy pattern or cosmic attunement to the four elements. In other words, the chart shows the various vibratory manifestations that comprise the individual's expression in this plane of creation, all of which follow a specific pattern of order which the chart symbolizes. In scientific terms, the chart shows your "energy field" or what clairvoyants call the "aura."

A Spiritual Perspective

In order to have the highest perspective possible in our efforts to understand the elements, it would be useful to refer to the writings of two of India's greatest spiritual teachers, both of whom Dr. Stone contacted in person and who have written extensively about the elements. Maharaj Charan Singh writes:

> All that we see with the physical eyes is made up of one or more of the five elements, namely, earth, water, air, fire, and ether; and all these five elements are inimical to each other. But with the help of, or due to, the soul, . . . all the five elements are contained and active in the human body, each one manifesting them according to his own karmas — in that proportion, but all the five elements are active, in a greater or lesser degree, in every human body.

He goes on to say that, when the soul leaves the body and this creation, the elements dissociate and return to their sources. It may be deduced that the Sun-sign in astrology is so important since it reveals the most basic attunement of the soul as it manifests on this plane of creation. It is similar to what the clairvoyant Edgar Cayce called "the personality of the soul."

Maharaj Sawan Singh writes that not only the body, but also the mind is "born of the finer essence of the five elements." In his writings, he correlates the elements with the lower chakras (or energy centers) in the body and with various qualities which have to be overcome for spiritual progress: air with greed; water with passion; fire with anger; and earth with attachment. A British writer and clairvoyant, Joan Cooke, has written a book called *Wisdom in the Stars* in which she likewise expresses the lessons of the elements that the soul must learn to evolve: fiery people need to learn love; watery people peace; air people brotherhood; and earthy people service.

The four elements are also the explanation for much of traditional occult doctrine, as can be clearly seen when the elements are correlated with the various "subtle bodies" or interpenetrating energy fields referred to so often in this field. Dr. Raynor Johnson, the author of many excellent books in the field of parapsychology such as *The Imprisoned Splendor* and *The Spiritual*

Path as well as a scientist of international repute, succinctly describes the nature of these subtler fields: "Surrounding the central reality are many vehicles or instruments or bodies — layers of consciousness which permit the individual to have relationships with many worlds or realms of being to which these vehicles are related." The elements are the vitalizing forces of each of these bodies. Water is correlated with the emotional or "astral" body, a type of consciousness dominated by intense yearnings, feeling reactions, and compelling desires. The element air is connected with the mental or "causal" body and represents a type of consciousness attuned to the abstract thought patterns of the universal mind. The earth element is symbolic of the physical body and of an attunement to the world of the physical senses and material forms. The fire element is correlated with the etheric or vital body, which acts as a transformer of the air and water energies to help support the functions of the physical body. The "vital" body is closely related to the physical body and is the same as the "etheric double" energy field so commonly reported in the investigations of parapsychologists.

The fact that the elements represent specific types of consciousness and perception and, as Dr. Raynor Johnson's quote indicates, that they reveal the ability to experience certain realms of being and to tune in to specific fields of life experience has important ramifications that will be dealt with in detail later in this book. First, however, we shall examine the elements in detail, in order to gain a deeper appreciation of what they represent.

Classification of Elements

The elements have traditionally been divided into two groups, fire and air being considered active and self-expressive, and water and earth considered passive, receptive, and self-repressive. These two groups are the same as the basic divisions of Chinese philosophy: yin (water and earth) and yang (air and fire). They are also identical with the Greek conception of two expressions of energy: Apollonian (fire and air, which actively and consciously form life) and Dyonisian (water and earth, which represent forces that manifest more unconsciously and instinctively). This differentiation is of great importance in a holistic approach to birthcharts, as we will see in the chapter on interpretation. I should emphasize here that we are dealing now with the basic principles alone and that a reference to water and earth, for example, as "self-repressive" or "unconscious" does not in any way indicate that people whose charts contain much emphasis on these elements are necessarily limited in awareness or particularly more "repressed" than any others. These terms refer more to the mode of operation of these energies and to the method of self-actualization than to a specific generalization which can be haphazardly applied to all people in a certain category. For example, the water and earth signs are more self-repressive than the fire and air signs in the sense that they live more within themselves and don't allow themselves to project their essential energy outwardly without a good deal of caution and forethought. The fire and air signs are more self-expressive since they are always "getting it out," pouring forth their energies and life-substance unreservedly: the fire signs by direct action and the air signs by social interaction and verbal expression.

Marc Edmund Jones, in an effort to classify the elements in a modern way that would not be misunderstood like the older terms "positive" and "negative," has written that air and fire are "manipulative and extensional" expressions of energy, whereas earth and water are "sustaining and intensive." Jones' definitions would be highly appropriate explanantions of the Greek terms *Apollonian* and *Dyonisian* as well. The elements fire and air have also been correlated with activity and with "levity," since air and fire tend to spread out and rise, extending toward a perimeter in space. Earth and water have been associated with "gravity" and inertia, since these elements tend to be under the influence of gravity and therefore to concentrate and collect at the lowest level. This classification of elements, and the fact that the signs of the same element and of the elements in the same group are considered to be generally "compatible," is of the greatest importance not only in the interpretation of individual charts but also in the art of chart comparison, with which we will deal later. It should also be pointed out that these principles of "levity," "gravity," and so forth are descriptive of a real flow of energy which may be perceived by those who are psychically sensitive, or at the very least felt in an immediate way by anyone relating closely to a person of different attunement.

The Element Fire

The element fire refers to a universal radiant energy, an energy which is excitable, enthusiastic, and which through its light brings color into the world. This element has been correlated with the dynamic core of psychic energy by C.G. Jung, that energy which flows spontaneously in an inspired, self-motivated way. Marc Edmund Jones equates fire with "experience centered in personal identity," and this explains why people with the fire signs dominant in their charts are so self-centered and usually rather impersonal. They feel themselves to be channels for "life" and they cannot easily hide their pride about this fact.

The fire signs exemplify high spirits, great faith in themselves, enthusiasm, unending strength, and a direct honesty. They need a great deal of freedom in order to express themselves naturally, and they usually ensure themselves that space by their unrelenting insistence on their point of view. Fire signs also are able to direct their will power consciously (although not always consistently) better than other signs. Their will to be and to express themselves freely is rather childlike in its simplicity, a quality which at times appears endearing to others but at other times seems offensive to those who are more cautious and sensitive. The faults of the fire signs rarely manifest as a result of bad intentions, but more often simply through a lack of self-control and sensitivity to others. They may come across as rather willful, even overpowering at times, rushing into things with such haste that they unintentionally cause destruction or hurt feelings in others.

The fire signs tend to be impatient with more sensitive or gentler people, especially those who are dominantly water and earth. The fire signs feel that water will extinguish it and that earth will smother it, and they often therefore resent the heaviness and emotionalism of these signs. The air signs, on the other hand, fan the flames of fire by providing new ideas that the fire sign person can act on. For this reason, fire is generally considered compatible with air, but it should be pointed out that the fire signs are often too flagrant and impatient for the delicate nervous system of the air signs to tolerate for long. In fact, although the fire signs will often be stimulated by the air signs, they easily become tired and bored with intellectual observations that can't be acted upon rather quickly.

The Element Air

The element air is the life-energy which has been associated with breath or what the yogis term "prana." The air realm is the world of archetypal ideas behind the veil of the physical world, the cosmic energy actualized into specific patterns of thought. It is associated with geometric lines of force functioning through the mind, the energy which shapes the patterns of things to come. Whereas the fire signs are concerned with *willing* something into being, the air signs focus their energy on specific ideas which have not yet materialized, and — by concentrating on these ideas — ensure that they eventually will materialize. Hence, although the air signs are often accused of being impractical dreamers, they are playing a part in the actualization of creation on the broadest social level, for their ideas can eventually touch the lives of millions of people.

Marc E. Jones writes that the air signs deal with "experience in its concern over theoretical relations." The emphasis on theory and on concepts in the life of air sign people leads to their finding the most compatible mode of expression in art, words, and abstract thought. The air signs have the ability to detach themselves from the immediate experience of daily life, thus enabling them to gain objectivity, perspective, and a rational approach in everything they do. This detachment also enables them to work effectively with all sorts of people, for they don't feel the need to get heavily involved with the other person's worries or emotions. The air signs are in fact the most social of all signs in the sense that they can objectively appreciate the other person's thoughts regardless of whether they agree with them.

Naturally, if the air signs become too occupied with their abstract ideas and theories, they can become mentally imbalanced and given to all sorts of eccentricity and fanaticism. They often lack deep emotion and an acceptance of the limitations of the physical body. They can over-value intellectual competence and refuse to face the fact that ideas must be tested to see if they work before they can be given great value. Thought is such a dominating force in the lives of air signs that they are most easily threatened if their opinions are ignored or the quality of their intellect disparaged. And, of course, the water and earth signs are the most likely to devalue the air signs' ideas, for those ideas don't usually meet the test of emotional depth or practicality that water and earth insist upon. For their part, the air signs don't want to be confined by the limitations of the earth, nor do they wish to have their light freedom saturated by the feelings and reservations of the water signs. Fire signs, on the other hand, stimulate the air signs toward more freedom of expresson and give the air signs a sense of confidence and strength that they can find with no one else. Although the air signs admire the fire signs in many ways, they will still insist upon their right to think things over before committing themselves, a habit that can become increasingly annoying to the fire signs.

The Element Water

Those with the water element strongly activated in their charts realize from birth that various intangible factors play a greater role in life than is commonly believed. The water signs are in touch with their feelings, in tune with the nuances and subtleties that many others don't even notice. The water element represents the realm of deep emotion and feeling responses, ranging from compulsive passions to overwhelming fears to an all-encompassing acceptance and love of creation. Since feelings by their very nature are partly unconscious, the water signs are simultaneously aware of the power of the unconscious mind and are themselves unconscious of much of what really motivates them. When they are in tune with the deeper dimensions of life with full awareness, they are the most intuitive, psychically sensitive signs. In that case, the water signs are in touch with the oneness of all creation and are able to help others by means of an empathetic responsiveness to the feelings of fellow beings. When, however, they are not fully aware of their own feelings, they find themselves prompted by compulsive desires, irrational fears, and great oversensitivity to the slightest threat.

The water signs, like the nature of water itself, have no solidity or shape of their own. They are therefore happiest when their fluidity is channeled and given form by someone else, particularly the earth signs who have the solidity that water can trust and rely on. The water signs tend to dislike those who are boisterous or who have strong personalities, such as the air and fire signs. They feel most comfortable with others who are rather secretive and self-contained, which gives them a greater feeling of protection and security. This secretive quality of the water signs, by the way, is rather deceptive; for, although they may be calm on the outside, there are constantly storms brewing on deeper levels and hidden undercurrents which can drag them down. In fact, the water signs can be sensationalistic at times, for they will unconsciously cultivate emotional storms and upheavals if their lives get too dreary.

The sensitivity of the water signs is so great and their vulnerability to hurt so pronounced that, if the emotional reactions are not controlled and channeled properly, it can lead to a state of emotional instability and a predisposition to being too easily influenced by the slightest wind that blows. The sensitivity of the water signs should not be considered weakness, however, for water has great force and penetrating power over a long period, especially when it is channeled in a concentrated way. A beautiful example of the power of this element is expressed by an 11th century Chinese scholar:

> "Of all the elements, the Sage should take water as his preceptor. Water is yielding but all-conquering. Water extinguishes Fire or, finding itself likely to be defeated, escapes as steam and reforms. Water washes away soft Earth or, when confronted by rocks, seeks a way around. . . .It saturates the atmosphere so that Wind dies. Water gives way to obstacles with deceptive humility, for no power can prevent it following its destined course to the sea. Water conquers by yielding; it never attacks but always wins the last battle." (from John Blofeld's *The Wheel of Life*, p. 78)

Lastly, the water element corresponds with the process of gaining consciousness through a slow but sure realization of the soul's deepest yearnings. The water signs know instinctively that they must protect themselves from outside influences in order to assure themselves the inner calm necessary for deep reflection and subtlety of perception. The realization of the true nature of their emotions and yearnings is a slow and often painful process, but as long as they are willing to face their real motives, they are assured of increasing inner contentment as the years pass.

The Element Earth

An attunement to this element indicates that the individual is in touch with the physical senses and the here-and-now reality of the material world. The earth signs tend to rely more upon their senses and practical reason than upon the inspirations, theoretical considerations, or intuitions of the other signs. They are attuned to the world of "forms" which the senses and practical mind regard as real, and their innate understanding of how the material world functions gives the earth signs more patience and self-discipline than other signs. They rarely have to be told how to fit into the world of making a living, supplying basic needs, and persisting till a goal is reached. All these qualities come naturally to those of the earth element.

Although the earth element is one of the passive or "receptive" elements, this element, like water, has strength of endurance and persistence that enables the earth signs always to look out for themselves. Although not particularly assertive, they will speak out when their "thing" is endangered or their security is threatened. And, due to their efficiency, they are apt not only to speak out but also to act in rather matter-of-fact ways to ensure that what they have worked for is not taken from them. The earth element tends to be cautious, premeditative, rather conventional, and unusually dependable. They are generally suspicious or dubious about more lively, agile-minded people, and they react to the air signs with some degree of reserve, although they may be somewhat fascinated by them. Nevertheless, they feel that the air signs are up in the clouds, playing childishly with impractical and unworkable schemes. They feel that the fire signs will parch the earth, storming through life much too quickly and forcefully to be trusted. The water signs, on the other hand, share their qualities of acquisitiveness, retentiveness, and self-protectiveness. The earth therefore feels that the water will refresh it and enable it to bring forth even more productivity.

The very attunement that supplies the earth signs with their power and special abilities can also be the source of their greatest faults. The involvement with the practical world can often limit their imagination if they rely too much on things as they are or as they appear to be. This can lead to a narrowness of outlook, an addiction to routine and order, and a total lack of ability to deal with the abstract and theoretical realms of activity. More than anything else, the earth signs need to open themselves to the reality of the unseen world and to commit themselves to specific ideals as guidelines for their activity.

11

Psychology of the Individual

The four elements are particularly useful in understanding the essential nature of any individual's psychological make-up. In order to approach this subject, let us here limit ourselves to a discussion of the element of the Sun sign only; for the element of the Sun sign is usually the dominant element in considering the overall psychology of the person. This is so because the Sun sign's element reveals the attunement of one's basic vitality and power of self-projection, as well as the realm of experience that the person *lives in* every day and the fundamental quality of his or her consciousness. (More than one element in a particular chart can be regarded as powerfully active, however, as we will discuss in a later chapter.)

The Sun sign element shows many things: it reveals "where you're coming from." In other words, it reveals where your consciousness is rooted, to what realm of experience you are attuned, and from what field of activity and being you derive your power. The Sun sign element also shows what is "real" to the individual, for it is the unconscious assumption of what is particularly real and what isn't that determines how the person will focus his energy. As an example, the air signs live in the abstract realm of thought, and a thought for them is just as real (indeed more real, as evidenced from their behavior) as any material object. The water signs live in their feelings, and it is their emotional state that determines their behavior more than anything else. The fire signs live in a state of highly excited, inspired activity; and maintaining that state of being is crucial for the fire signs to stay healthy and happy. The earth signs are grounded in the material world. The material world and its considerations for survival and production are considered much more real than any other aspect of life.

Another way of expressing this same differentiation is to say that the element of one's Sun sign reveals the basic inner force motivating everything we do. The air signs are motivated by their intellectual *concepts,* the water signs by their deepest emotional *yearnings,* the fire signs by their *inspirations* and *aspirations*, and the earth signs by their material *needs.* If only psychologists, psychiatrists, and counselors of various sorts would learn this basic classification of personality types, they would take a great step forward in their efforts to unravel the endlessly complex forces at work in human motivation and behavior.

The element of the Sun sign also gives us insight into how any individual sees life (i.e., the quality of their overall perception) and what expectations they have of life experience. In his *Encyclopedia of Psychological Astrology,* C.E.O. Carter has concisely expressed the psychological bias of each element in words that are worth repeating here. For the fire signs, he says that the self is felt as a "projection of the Life-Principle into Nature and acting upon it" and that these signs seek "experiences of a positive kind in the field of action." For the water signs, the self, projected into nature, is conceived as "likely to suffer and need protection." He points out that the water signs help to preserve life by "entering into the feelings of others" and that this ability to tune in on others' feelings can be a "helpful guardian or a cunning enemy."

The earth signs, according to Carter, see nature as a "field for the manifestation of life" and, through their instinctive attunement to the material world, they are able to help sustain life through the utilization and mastery of natural processes. For the air signs, nature is perceived as "something to be understood, as well as utilized, the understanding being the condition for complete and correct utilization." The airy mental principle is used therefore to improve life by giving one a perspective on spontaneous natural processes. The complementary nature of the air and earth principles is symbolized clearly by the joint rulership of Venus, Mercury and Saturn over the signs of these two elements.

When approached on the level of energy attunement alone, we come across some rather startling insights into the nature of the Sun sign element. Throughout his biography *Born to Heal*, the man called Mr. A whom we mentioned earlier repeatedly refers to the need that each of us has to "feed" his or her energy field. If we neglect to recharge our basic Sun sign energy (as well as the energies indicated by the elemental placement of the other planets and ascendent), we find ourselves becoming depleted, irritable, and more vulnerable to physical and psychological disturbances. We can accomplish this feeding in a number of ways: through intensive relationship (which we will deal with later), through tuning in consciously to the required energies, or through specific types of activities and involvements in everyday life. The Sun sign element represents the most important requirement for refueling since that is the primary energy that we are constantly depleting. In *Born to Heal*, Mr. A is quoted repeatedly concerning the serious consequences of allowing ourselves to become devitalized of our necessary element fuel.

We have all heard of a person being "out of his element," in other words someone dealing with a realm of activity which is alien to his true nature. For example, an airy person trying to deny his intellectual needs and make his living as a laborer would likely be out of his element. If this person didn't compensate by engaging in social or intellectual activities when he was off work, he would gradually exhaust himself because his air element would not be getting recharged. In other words, the element of one's Sun sign is the fuel that you need to feel alive! It is the source of our basic vitality and the power which enables us to revitalize ourselves in order to cope with the stresses and demands of daily life. Although theoretically one could compensate for spending the majority of one's time in a type of work that was "out of his element," any individual must find a type of work that is truly of his element if that vocation is going to be fulfilling over a long period of years.

In a general way, we can recharge our batteries by involving ourselves in activities that supply us with the necessary fuel. The water signs therefore need dealings with other watery people or intense emotional involvement with whatever they are doing. These people cannot be detached from their experience, so it is important that they choose activities and work that allow them a full scope for their emotional expression. The fire signs require involvement with other fiery people, with promotional, inspired goals and aspirations, or with a type of work that is physically demanding and active. The earth signs need to take on material duties and obligations, for the challenges of coping with the world at large stimulate their best energies and feed their need to express themselves through practical accomplishment. They may also recharge themselves by dealing closely with other earthy types of people. The air signs feel the need for regular relationship with other people of like mind, for social involvements that allow them a channel for the expression of their ideas, or for a type of work that gives them intellectual freedom and stimulation.

One can also consciously tune in on the required energy by cultivating close physical contact with that element; for, in a real way, the earth signs get their energy from the earth, the air signs get their power from the air, the water signs from the flow of watery feelings or from contact with water itself, and the fire signs from the Sun and physical activity. Anyone who doubts the truth of this statement has obviously not experienced its reality in his own life. Clairvoyants with especially refined perception have told me that they could see the rootedness in the earth of a Taurus, the rock-like groundedness of a Capricorn, a smooth flow of feeling sensitivity like a waterfall in Cancers, the sudden change of polarity similar to electrical storms in Aquarius, and so forth. One can therefore take advantage of contact with one's Sun sign element for the purpose of rejuvenation and recuperation from the devitalizing impact of life's demands.

In order to do this, the earth signs naturally need to get their feet in the mud once in a while, to get close to nature, and to tune in on the power of growth in trees and plants. To give an example of this, I once knew a double Taurus person who had no knowledge of astrology but who had found that she gained the greatest peace and tranquility by going to a nearby river to play in the mud for hours. The air signs need clean, thin, highly electric air for their recuperation, a quality of atmosphere that is never found in our cities or humid plains or agricultural valleys. This type of air is available particularly in the mountains, where it is not only clean but also rather dry and crisp. An Aquarius doctor friend of mine says that he believes that the best altitutde for air signs is at least one half mile above sea level, and he himself lives at such an altitude for that reason.

The water signs usually feel that living too far from a river, lake, or ocean is like living in a sterile desert. They are at their best psychically and emotionally when they have the opportunity to either immerse themselves in flowing water regularly or at the very least to be in the presence of water. Some readers may recall that Edgar Cayce, the great American clairvoyant, found that his psychic faculties operated more effectively when he lived near water, a fact which led to his moving near the ocean to Virginia Beach. Cayce's Sun was in Pisces, and his psychic readings are replete with references to the beneficial effects of being near water for psychic or metaphysical work.

The fire signs need to be outdoors in the sunshine, soaking in the radiant fire from the sun. They also need to remain physically active in order to tap into their fiery energy. A fire sign who has to remain cooped up for very long or who does not have the opportunity for *vigorous* physical movement soon begins to feel like he's dying. This is the reason that a debilitating illness or accident for the fire signs so often has such serious psychological consequences. Many readers have probably noticed that all the fire signs seem to have their peak energy while the sun is up, whereas they don't know what to do with themselves after dark. This fire energy can also be stored up during the summer months, to be used later during colder weather. I remember one Leo woman telling me that she was never sick during winter if she had been out in the sun a great deal the previous summer. However, during one summer, she had to remain indoors virtually all the time due to her work; and the following winter found her constantly ill.

Psychologist Ralph Metzner is one of the few in his field who has studied the elements as they relate to personality types. While at Stanford University, Metzner designed small encounter sessions between people of various element combinations. After some experience with these experiments and after studying the astrological correlations with the elements in some depth, Metzner concluded tht the four elements symbolize types of people who "metabolize experience at different rates" and in different ways. These different approaches to experience lead these four types of people to deal with conflicts or obstacles in their lives in different ways. The air signs tend to rise above conflict and to float around it. Although they may later resent the person who put the problem in their path, they will at the time rarely fail to deal with it gracefully. The water signs also detest all form of conflict (with the exception of some Scorpios). They tend to flow around it, under it, over it, or — if all else fails — to slowly wear away the person or thing in their path. Scorpio, however, often seeks out challenges and problems, subliminally realizing that such challenges call forth their greatest strength and resources. Still, Scorpio most of the time will maintain a pregnant silence, not wanting to cause unnecessary conflict.

The earth signs, being rather solid by nature, tend to disdain conflict, preferring to slowly absorb the brunt of the problem. However, if they are driven back against a wall, they are capable of hitting the obstacle hard with full force. This is particularly true of Taurus, the fixed earth, who will never seek out conflicts but who is capable of surprising power and anger if pushed too far. The fire signs tend to overpower obstacles, to burn them up, or to scare them away through show of force. They rarely display behavior that could be termed tactful. Lois H. Sargent, in her excellent book on chart comparisons *How to Handle Your Human Relations*, gives great importance to the elements as a means of understanding how different people approach problem-solving. She writes that the fire signs respond to situations with intensity, "desiring direct action in the solving of problems, and tending more to impulse than deliberation. The earth types are motivated by the desire for practical, useful results. They usually have sound common sense, whether they use it or not. The air sign people like to reason things out and generally think before they act. The water sign types are impressionable, sensitive, and intuitive. They incline to wait on circumstances for guidance in solving problems."

An understanding of the elements can, as we have seen, contribute to self-knowledge in many ways, showing us how we can best live with ourselves, fulfill our needs, and revitalize our energy field. The elements also give us an indication of how we can advantageously control and channel our energies. The medieval physician-astrologer Paracelsus, a man whom Jung considered a forerunner to modern psychologists, attributed a specific nature spirit to each of the elements. These spirits, or their variations, are found throughout mythology worldwide and symbolize graphically how the elements operate. This is not the place to dwell on the question of how "real" such spirits are, but a brief reference to the writings of Paracelsus here sheds light on how we can work with these forces. The *undines* were considered the spirits of water, and Paracelsus stated that they must be controlled by firmness. Hence, we can learn that watery people need to be firm with themselves and also that firmness is often the best way to deal with this type of person, especially when their emotions are out of control. The spirits of the air were said to be the *sylphs*, and they could be controlled through constancy. It is clear that a defininte, consistent approach to life is something that the air signs could well cultivate. Making a commitment with determined resolution is difficult for the air signs, but it is an important step in their evolution.

The spirits of the fire are the *salamanders*, and they can be controlled chiefly through placidity. In other words, the fire signs can curb the extreme uses of their energy by consciously cultivating a tranquil, placid state of contentment. If the fire signs can learn this art of calmly accepting life in the here and now, they would avoid a great deal of stress and wasted energy. The earth spirits are the *gnomes*, which are to be controlled by cheerful generosity. Obviously, cheerful generosity is not a quality commonly found in the earth signs, and it is therefore something they can all benefit from learning. And, I might add, the greatest strength and radiance of the earth signs shines forth when they have assimilated this quality into their nature.

The Elements in the Healing Arts

This is not the place to go into great detail on the function of the elements in various healing arts, but it is worth mentioning in order to give a different perspective on the living reality of these forces. In fact, it is by direct experience with the flow of the elements, such as one can find through their use in the healing arts, that we can most obviously perceive their power and impact at every level of life. I have already mentioned how Mr. A used the basic life forces in his healing work, and readers should refer to *Born to Heal* for more extensive treatment of his ideas. Dr. Stone's work has also been referred to, and a full treatment of his therapeutic system called "Polarity Therapy" would take many volumes. More than any other Western physician, Dr. Stone has outlined a complete science of the four elements in a way that makes these forces accessible to treatment when they become imbalanced. Although Dr. Stone has written a number of books,* most of them are too technical for the layman. He does, however, have a couple volumes that are fairly easy for anyone to understand, *Energy: The Vital Principle in the Healing Art* being the most thorough explanation of the elements. (See Appendix C for a more complete explanation of Polarity Therapy and its relation to astrology.)

Many of Dr. Stone's ideas were derived from Indian Ayurvedic Medicine, a very ancient system of healing based entirely on the relationship of the elements to foods, weather, exercise, medicines, and various types of activities. Chinese acupuncture is another type of healing art based on the theory of elements, and anyone getting a treatment of this type can experience the reality of extremely potent energy flow, as the specific points are stimulated in order to free the specific energy current (or "meridian") that was blocked or imbalanced. Those who study Hatha Yoga will also encounter the theory of the elements and their correlations with specific energy centers (or "chakras") found along the spine, and those who practice this yoga consistently can experience the reality of the elements in their own life with great immediacy. Dr. William Davidson, whose *Lectures on Medical Astrology* are well worth reading, was a homeopathic physician who lectured extensively about the importance of the elements. In his published lectures one may find mention of various physiological problems that come about due to an emphasis on a particular element in the natal chart.

All of these therapeutic systems are based upon a similar idea: that the elements are the vital forces that enliven us at every level. As the 19th Century American herbalist Samuel Thomson wrote:

---

*Dr. Stone's writings are now collected into three books. *Health Building* details a complete health program, including exercise and diet. *Polarity Therapy: The Complete Collected Works* are available in a two-volume set totaling 576 pages, complete with hundreds of charts and diagrams. Volume I is the best introduction to Polarity Therapy for the new student. Write the publisher of this book for information and current prices.

All bodies are composed of four elements — Earth, Air, Fire, and Water. The healthy state consists in the proper balance and distribution of these four elements, and disease is their derangement.

The Medieval-Renaissance theory of the four humors (choler or yellow bile, blood, phlegm, and black bile) was based on a similar notion and related to the elements of astrology. The theory was that when these four humours were mixed in exactly the right proportions in an individual, he would be healthy and have a well-balanced personality. A slight predominance of one humour or element (which we all have, according to our natal charts) was considered to affect not only a man's physical characteristics but also his complexion and temperament. The remnants of these old beliefs are still found in our language, for the very word *complexion* means "entwined together" and the word *temperament* is derived from the Latin *temperamentum*, meaning "a mixing in proportions."

These ancient concepts were ridiculed by most scientists and physicians until recently, when the rediscovery of oriental healing methods and the renaissance of herbal and homeopathic methods have forced the open-minded members of these groups to take another look at long neglected ideas. If indeed we are composed of these four basic energies, it makes sense to relate treatment of specific ailments to the element attunement of the individual. One modern physician who has begun to delve into this subject is Dr. Aubrey T. Westlake, M.D., the author of *The Pattern of Health*. In his book, Dr. Westlake states that "disease in its origin is not material," but rather that it results from an interference with the free and unimpeded flow of the basic life energies, with a consequent "damming block, cutting off, alteration and distortion" of the energies. Only then, he writes, do certain conditions of deficiency, imbalance, overgrowth, etc. arise, and we call them disease. Dr. Westlake calls the elements the "formative ethers" and says that "the free flow and harmonious and balanced interaction of all these forces constitutes what we have called the state of health or wholeness." In words closely paralleling those of Dr. Stone's writings, Dr. Westlake continues:

Never before did we know so much about disease and pathological conditions — and so little about health and wholeness. Modern Medicine is indeed in a vicious circle, and there is no escape
so long as we continue to think in purely materialistic terms. To
escape from the impasse it is essential to begin to recognize that
there are in fact forces which lie behind the manifestations of
matter.

What does all this have to do with astrology? It is simply that,
through the use of astrology with a proper understanding of the
workings of the basic energies (or elements), we can ascertain
which elements are excessive, lacking, or imbalanced or which
ones are likely to be the source of problems, physically and mentally. As Dr. Westlake writes:

Here for the first time we have the possibility of a true preventa-
tive medicine, as we can now detect these deviations from the
norm before they have manifested physically, at which early
stage they are eminently treatable, or become set in a pattern
which we know as pathological disease, when they are not.

12

Elements in Interpretation

The interpretation of astrological charts takes on a new and deeper meaning when emphasis is put upon the elements; for in this way one is dealing with the specific life energies at work rather than concentrating only on the manifestations of these energies in outward behavior and personality characteristics. As we have stated before, every individual is, so to speak, composed of all four elements. A human being cannot exist if even one of the elements is missing, for he would then be totally devoid of the function of that energy both psychologically and physically. However, the elements most emphasized in a natal chart by planetary placement and the element of the Ascendant indicate the chief energies and qualities to which one is attuned *consciously*. Such dominant elements show what you're "in touch with" and therefore what energies you are capable of utilizing rather easily in your everyday life, as well as in what realms of experience you can participate naturally and spontaneously. Elements that are lacking emphasis in the chart indicate specific realms of life activity with which one is not consciously in contact, and hence these elements reveal an attunement which must be consciously cultivated and developed in order to afford the individual the minimal participation in that field of experience required for a full and well-rounded life.

A great deal may be learned about a person simply by analyzing any marked imbalance of the elements in the individual's chart. It is very common to find in this way a particular life problem that has perplexed the person (whether consciously or unconsciously) throughout life, and the increased awareness of his innate imbalance can appreciably help him to cultivate a more meaningful contact with areas of experience which previously had been alien to him. Naturally, one cannot change one's attunement simply through analysis and discussion of the prob-

lem, but one can begin to realize more fully the fact that there are
fields of activity and types of people which can teach the individual something which he vitally needs. Likewise, those who
have an over-emphasis on a particular element in the natal chart
tend to over-value that realm of experience, to the detriment of
their potential for wholeness.

When analyzing a chart in terms of balance of the elements, the
most dominant element is usually — but not always — that of the
Sun sign. Second in importance are the elements of the Moon,
Ascendant, and Mars. And lastly, the elements of Venus and
Mercury, followed in order of importance by Jupiter and Saturn.
The elements of Uranus, Neptune, and Pluto have very little to do
with the *conscious* attunement of the individual, although they do
indicate unconscious factors motivating the whole generation of
people to which that individual belongs. However, for all practical
purposes, the elements indicated by the placement of the trans-
Saturnian planets should be disregarded in such an evaluation. I
should add that the element of the planet that rules the Ascendant, as well as the element of the Sun sign's ruler, is given added
emphasis unless the ruling planet is Uranus, Neptune, or Pluto.
If one has Scorpio rising, for example, the element of Mars would
be given more emphasis, but not that of Pluto, Scorpio's co-ruler.
The elemental placement of the Ascendant's ruler in particular is
of such vital importance and has such a power of attunement in
the individual's life that one should always regard that element
as strongly accented. For example, someone with Libra rising and
with Venus in Cancer, but with no other planets in water signs,
would be strongly influenced by and would overtly express many
of the qualities associated with the water element. In other words,
such a person would be forcefully motivated by emotional needs,
the urge to express sensitive feelings and affections, and the sympathetic nature of Cancer. This would be true even if the Sun and
Moon, as well as the Ascendant, are in air signs.

Focusing on the element of the Ascendant's ruler provides the
practitioner with an insight into one of the primary motivating
urges of the individual, an insight that could easily be missed if
one merely adds up the number of planets in each element and
gives them equal weight in determining the dominant elemental

attunement. The practice just mentioned is used haphazardly by many astrologers, and the resulting inaccuracy of their judgments based on this practice impels them to look for all sorts of "esoteric" reasons to explain the observed characteristics of the person they're dealing with. As always in the practice of astrology, if one truly learns the basics and *understands* their dynamic function on the level of energy expression, he or she will rarely have to rely on any of the myriad of secondary techniques commonly praised by their proponents.

An example of the strength of the elemental placement of the Sun sign's ruler can further clarify this method of procedure. I recently did a chart for a woman with the Sun, Moon, Venus, Uranus, Jupiter, and Mercury all in the sign Aries. Naturally, one would correctly assume that such a person would exemplify fiery characteristics. However, unless one payed attention to the fact that Aries' ruler Mars is in Pisces (and this is the *only* planet in a water sign), it would be easy to describe this person as insensitively self-centered in the typical Aries way. The fact that the "dispositor" of all the Aries planets is in a water sign, however, tempers the expression of the fiery Arian drive and colors the person's self-expression with a sensitivity not usually found in someone with all these planets in Aries.

In analyzing the balance or imbalance of the elements in an individual's chart, therefore, one should not be too hasty in making generalizations. One chart factor can alter the expression of the whole energy field, and I strongly advocate for this reason that astrologers who merely add up the number of planets in each element should take another look at this practice and honestly face its limitations and proneness toward unjustifiable conclusions. The ideal to look for in evaluating the elemental emphasis in a chart is at least some attunement to each element. This results in the ability to achieve a balanced approach to living and the capacity to participate immediately in all the realms of experience. Naturally, very few people have this ideal balance, and the lack of it should not be judged as a necessarily negative feature of the person's approach to life. People are capable of compensating for their lacks and weaknesses, and they can consciously cultivate the qualities and attunements which they lack at birth. The balance of the elements should be seen more as a guideline for further growth, therefore, than as a factor necessarily limiting their lifelong self-expression.

Imbalance of Fire

If one has too little emphasis in the fire signs, the fiery energy is lacking and the digestion is likely to be weak. A lack of fire usually manifests as a lack of spiritedness, a tendency not to trust life itself. The joy of living is often markedly absent, and the person is often devoid of faith and optimism. Self-confidence may also be poor, and there is often a tendency towards despondency and lack of enthusiasm for meeting life's demands. Challenges often scare these people, and any major life problem takes a long while to overcome, since the residual psychological effects tend to linger long after the experience has reached its peak. A lack of fire is almost always indicative of a major problem in the way the person approaches life. Vigorous physical exercise tends to stimulate the fiery energy and is highly recommended for this type of person. The diet should also be watched carefully, especially if the person also lacks earth, for he then doesn't have the digestive strength to burn up heavy, concentrated foods. Everything, including exercise and dietary habits, should be done with moderation so that the person doesn't exhaust what energy he has. These people often, however, have great patience, and strong Mars or Sun emphasis may somewhat compensate.

Too much emphais on fire is rarely felt to be a problem by the individual until it is too late to do anything about it. This could manifest as "burning yourself out," leaving an exhausted shell of a person, especially if alcohol or drugs are abused. They tend to be overly active, restless, and overly concerned with making something happen in the world. Too much fire can also lead to problems in dealing with others, for the impulsiveness, self-centeredness, and unrestrained desire to act directly at all costs can give rise to an extremely insensitive, crude way of approaching other people. (This could be off-set if there is a good deal of water or air in the chart.) C.E.O. Carter evaluates this imbalance in the following terms:

Under affliction this force becomes uncontrolled and causes those under its influence to be wild, turbulent, given to extravagance and exaggeration, passionate and reckless, over-confident and self-indulgent. We get primitive traits, and marked tendency to ego-exaltation, self-importance, vanity, and love of pomp and grandeur.

At best, those attuned strongly to fire are self-motivated go-getters, and often successfully start and promote new enterprises, projects, and idealistic ventures that demand trememdous dedication, courage, and energy.

Imbalance of Earth

Those having too little emphasis on the earth element are not naturally attuned to the physical world, the physical body, or to the limitations and requirements of survival in the material plane. They can therefore be "spaced out," since they are not grounded in the here and now realization of their dependence on material things such as food, money, shelter, and other practical considerations. Such a person is often able to ignore the requirements of surviving in the material world and tends to fight "growing up" and accommodating himself to harsh necessities until he is forced to do so by the impinging demands of the reality he'd prefer to ignore. This lack of contact with the material world and with the physical dimension of reality can lead to the person feeling totally out of place in this world, with no grounding or rootedness to provide him with support and solidity in his efforts to express himself. He often feels like he has no place to stand, doesn't fit into any niche in society's structure, and often has trouble finding a life's work that is satisfying. This feeling of being out of place in the world often leads these people to a search for direct experience with some dimension of life that seems more real to them, such as being active in the world of imagination or pursuing a spiritual quest in order to transcend the limitations of the material world once and for all. In other words, this lack of earth can have some very beneficial effects, for the person accepts no limitations to what is possible, either spiritually or in his creative efforts. The imagination can run wild, and this can at times lead to fruitful results, but only if the individual has at least learned to accept the basic requirements of earthly living.

A lack of earth can also lead to ignoring the requirements of the physical body. Their physical needs seem to them rather secondary, if indeed they are considered at all; and hence, they often forget to eat, exercise, and rest at regular intervals. One often finds a poor skin tone, an indication that the life energy is not strongly vitalizing the physical vehicle, whereas those with a great emphasis on earth often have especially oily and active skin with good tone and color. Those with a lack of earth can benefit immeasurably by consciously cultivating a regular schedule in their lives, setting aside definite periods for eating in a relaxed way, exercising moderately, and getting sufficient rest. In other words, by consciously accepting the limitations of the physical world, they can master it and make use of the sustaining power of the earth. It may be useful to mention here that, although one may lack earth sign emphasis in his chart, strong aspects with Saturn can in many ways off-set the problematical side of this imbalance.

Those with too great an emphasis on the earth element tend to rely too much on things as they are or as they appear to be. There can be a narrowness of vision, an obsessive concern with what "works" rather than with what ideals one should shoot for, and often a marked lack of imagination. Former President Nixon is a good example (with Virgo rising and Capricorn Sun) of someone who over-emphasized practical efficiency and material concerns to the detriment of theoretical and ethical principles. It is easy for these people to lose perspective on their actions (unless they have an emphasis on air to balance this) and on the ultimate implications of their methods of operation. Naturally, those with a great deal of attunement to earth will exemplify a remarkable strength and efficiency in most cases, and they need to channel their energy into a specific work that challenges them. However, the world of work and practical affairs often tends to dominate their entire lives, with the eventual result that their entire sense of self-worth is threatened when there is an unforeseen change in their vocational activities. There is often a particular cynicism and skepticism present in these people, qualities of mind which inevitably arise if one has no ideal or inspiration to infuse life with significance. A strong emphasis on Neptune or, to some extent, Jupiter can help the person to channel his practicality in a way that enables him to transcend the more negative qualities of this imbalance.

Imbalance of Air

Those with too little emphasis on the air element in their charts rarely perceive this to be a problem, for they are too involved in action, feelings, and material concerns to consider the implications of their involvements. However, it is just this lack of perception, this inability to reflect on life and one's self that creates problems for these people. It is difficult for them to achieve detachment from their personal actions, and hence they often find themselves burdened by involvements that were not sufficiently considered beforehand or by a lack of satisfaction in close relationships stemming from their inability to cooperate effectively. The element air is a unifying quality and enables one to adjust easily and quickly to new ideas and different sorts of people. Those who lack this attunement naturally have difficulty adjusting themselves to new ideas, and therefore to new people. This can lead to a distrust of anyone who seems too "intellectual." A good example of this type is Governor Wallace, whose chart emphasizes mainly fire and earth. His campaigns in the past have been noted for constant criticism of "pointy-headed intellectuals." In other words, these people often distrust others who seem to think too much. A strong Mercury emphasis can to some extent off-set this imbalance.

An attunement to air indicates that one can easily see things in a certain perspective, but those who lack this attunement have difficulty getting a perspective on themselves and can't reflect easily from an objective viewpoint. They don't analyze themselves as a rule (unless Virgo is emphasized to off-set this) and they are rarely known for their reasoning power and articulate way of expressing themselves. At times, the nervous system is weak and the lack of ability to adjust quickly to new ideas can in some cases cause psychosomatic problems. These people can have violent reactions if they hear an idea that they can't assimilate mentally and emotionally. Their physical reaction to unassimilable ideas or to new types of people jolts them to such an extent that they either get physically ill or lash out irrationally in an effort to eliminate the source of this threatening thought.

Those with too much emphasis on the air element have an over-active mind which must be guided and controlled. This is the sort of person to "lives in his head" and, if there is little earth or fire to motivate him to act on the ideas, he can become a dabbler in all sorts of curiosities without having much effect or developing much depth within himself. These people can't do anything without thinking about it first, which can lead in extreme cases to a paralysis of will and severe psychological disorders. The mind can run away with them, leading them at times into a world of imagination and conceptual brilliance but at other times to a sense of "reality" totally out of touch with what is possible. With proper mental discipline, this type of person can be an innovator in the world of thought. (Witness the fact that more Nobel Prize winners have had the Sun in air signs than any other element.) He often has special abilities for coordinating activities with diverse sorts of people.

Physically, this type of person can be so out of touch with his body that he allows the mind to run away with him until he is utterly exhausted. The nervous system is highly activated and extremely sensitive, but these people exhaust their nervous energy more quickly than others since they are using it more. A restful period of recuperation or meditation is necessary to allow the nervous system to recharge itself and to keep the mind from driving them to a state of psychic exhaustion. It is necessary for these people to have a periodic change of scenery away from their usual work and domestic duties to allow the mind to get out of its deep rut of worries, second thoughts, and endless plans

Imbalance of Water

Too little emphasis on the element water can manifest as a wide range of psychological, emotional, and physical problems. Most people with a lack of watery attunement have great difficulty entering into the feelings of others with empathy and compassion, as well as getting in touch with their own feelings and emotional needs. This does not mean that they lack sensitivity in all cases, but they inevitably have trouble dealing with their own feelings; the world of emotions seems to them a foreign land of great peril which would likely be more troublesome than beneficial. In extreme cases, one finds cold, aloof, and callous people with this imbalance. Such people are noted for their lack of sympathy and rarely have good emotional rapport with others. They tend to disregard the feelings of others as unimportant, unable to see in others that which they cannot accept in themselves. In their attempt to be emotionally self-sufficient, they often deny their emotional nature altogether, which can lead to a particularly unconscious dependency on others who do express feelings.

A lack of the water element also manifests as an innate distrust of intuitive knowledge. In fact, in some cases, these people's chief emotional problem is that they don't trust themselves at all since they readily dismiss their feelings as unimportant annoyances. As Jung pointed out in all of his writings, however, whatever is denied conscious access continues to influence the individual anyhow, but via unconscious processes. People lacking water will very often resist all efforts of others to draw them out of their emotional void, while at the same time making groping, half-conscious gestures towards others which reveal their loneliness, fear, or inner misery. Those with this imbalance in their charts can achieve a measure of emotional stability by slowly letting the seemingly endless pool of feelings come to the surface, thus releasing the accumulated pain and suffering which they have for so long denied. These people seem fanatically fearful of pain, with the result that their disregard of their emotional needs insures that they will experience more pain.

On the physical level, a lack of water almost always manifests as a rather severe physical disturbance, usually due in great part to excess toxicity. The water element is the cleansing, healing, purging energy, and those who lack it allow themselves to be slowly poisoned by the simultaneous accumulation of emotional and physical waste products. Such a toxic condition can express itself through an endless variety of symptoms, but the therapy required is generally the same for all: a complete physical and emotional purging. Dr. Stone, whom we mentioned earlier, stated in lecture that 90 to 95% of physical problems involve the water element and therefore the emotional side of the nature. Those in whom the water element is not operating efficiently are particularly prone to physical symptoms of disease. The fact that the watery energy is the cleansing and healing force is evident in the great preponderance of water signs in the charts of most natural healers. The diet of those lacking water should be watched carefully, and they can greatly benefit from periodic cleansing diets or moderate fasts. In other words, when these people consciously work at augmenting the cleansing function on the emotional and physical levels, they are able to overcome many of these problems and to avoid most of the severe disturbances to which such a toxic state would eventually lead.

Those with an over-emphasis on the water element may feel like they are cast adrift on the open sea in a small boat with no rudder, no sail, no oar, and no compass. They are usually rather easily influenced by any wind that blows, making them overly impressionable and often times at the mercy of emotional patterns over which they have no control. Most people with this imbalance are extremely sensitive to any experience, which can lead either to profoundly penetrating intuition or to *over*-reacting to the slightest stimulus. If the emotions are totally out of control and if the person habitually functions in a state of apprehensive self-protectiveness, he can easily become devitalized by fears, negative reaction patterns, and timidity. Being overwhelmed by emotions as a daily life experience ultimately wears out anyone, and the fact that these people often feel unable to cope with the stresses of dealing with the outer world can prompt them to withdraw into their inner life or to run away from life's challenges.

These people can in fact be "water-logged" with emotions and contradictory feelings, a state of affairs most likely to come about if they are not using their feeling sensitivity and empathy in an active concern for others. At their best, once the self-absorption has been overcome, these people are capable of developing an emotional self-sufficiency based upon a rich inner life of total dedication to an ideal. They often have pronounced imaginative abilities and a natural attunement to spiritual and occult realities. Their seemingly absolute dedication to a life of self-sacrifice is often genuine, but in others this is simply a guise veiling an absolute selfishness and a compulsive pattern of demanding that others fill up their inner emptiness. There is no way to understand this type of person unless one realizes that they are motivated chiefly by deep yearnings and insecurities which they have difficulty identifying. Until these yearnings are clarified in the full light of consciousness, these people cannot help but be rather compulsive in their behavior. And, until the yearnings are identified as the soul's desire for liberation and ultimate serenity, the individual cannot effectively make use of his greatest strength.

More than with any other element, those with too much water emphasis tend to go to extremes of behavior, and it is difficult therefore to make generalizations that will hold true for all people of this category. It is evident to me, however, that those with this combination in their charts have the potential for expressing fully the highest spiritual qualities: love, compassion, devotion, and sympathetic helpfulness. Those who have achieved this level of self-expression are, however, decidedly in the minority. On the physical level, a great emphasis on the water element indicates that the body is always eliminating poisons, both physical toxins and emotional residue. The efficiency of this cleansing process, however, depends on how aware the person is of his emotional needs.

Self-Expressive or Self-Repressive Emphasis

As mentioned in the section on the classification of the elements, the active or self-expressive elements (air and fire) and the passive or self-repressive elements (water and earth) form two distinct types of energy attunement. In an individual chart, one often finds that one of these two types is over-emphasized and the other is considerably lacking. This gives rise to specific psychological imbalances, particularly evident when the elements are classified as conscious (air and fire) and unconscious (water and earth). Therefore, it would be useful here to anlayze briefly how such imbalances are expressed and what particular psychological characteristics are accordingly indicated.

Over-Emphasis on Water & Earth
Lack of Air & Fire

The strongest characteristics of this type are a profound depth, seriousness, and self-protectiveness in all activities. They are usually hard workers and in fact don't feel comfortable if they are not bearing some burden, either emotionally or in their everyday work. They are very conscious of survival needs, security needs, and others' reliance on their solidity and resources. Hence, much of their energy is utilized in an effort to maintain their resources and a great attachment to money, possessions, job, children, and other security factors often results. They have a strength of endurance and an ability to survive through any calamity. Their attachment to security and to rather traditional values is often manifested in a strong adherence to family, home, and community responsibilities.

The problematical side of this type can be understood when it is seen that these people are motivated chiefly by feelings, fears, habits, past conditioning, security needs, and other unconscious factors. This often gives rise to a tendency to manipulate others in order to fulfill their own security needs and to be too attached to the past and rather fearful of the present and future. There is often a vital lack of ideals, faith, and positive thinking, and their intellectual and communicative faculties are usually underdeveloped. At best, this type is grounded in the here and now reality of everyday experience and faces things with great inner strength and determination. At worst, they can be stingy, manipulative, greedy, and ultimately deeply frustrated in their need to take some risks to promote their growth.

Over-Emphasis on Air & Fire
Lack of Water & Earth

This type at best represents an idealistic, aspiring, positive-thinking person whose intentions and motives are above reproach. Their approach to life is not particularly realistic, however, and they often find that they must learn about the darker side of life through hard experience and disillusionment. They often neglect the very needs and feelings which can give them more stability and inner strength. Those with this emphasis, however, often gravitate (by way of compensation) to the study of the unconscious, emotional problems, and how to take care of physical necessities. This is a marked step in their growth toward a more comprehensive way of life. This type of person has the ability to put his ideas into action and the capacity to gain a perspective on the meaning and implication of his actions. The danger with this emphasis is that the person will live in his head and in his aspirations and thereby neglect the emotional depth and physical needs from which he could derive inner resources.

This type is known for a keen sense of humor, an optimistic approach to life, and often a marked verbal ability. At best, this is an exceptionally creative combination, harmonizing ideas, inspirations, and plans with the ability and drive to execute them. The problem with really getting things done, however, comes from the fact that this person is not *grounded;* they would rather stay high, rising above the more mundane necessities of dealing with responsibilities, emotional needs, and persistent work. They can therefore scatter their energy and over-extend themselves until they are burnt out and exhausted. The lack of depth and sustaining power makes it difficult for them to recharge their batteries in an effort to recuperate from everyday stresses. The rejuvenating, healing qualities of earth and water are lacking in this person; they therefore need to realize that they can't just pour out their energies unreservedly without simultaneously tuning in on their deeper resources if they are to avoid a state of constant depletion.

Other Element Combinations

The other combinations of two elements within one person are comprised of "incompatible" energies. This can obviously make for certain problems of integration, for such different types of energies represent two different and alien dimensions of life which are able to be focused simultaneously only with the greatest effort, discipline, and practice. In extreme cases, the individual will feel pulled toward two radically different modes of self-expression, with a feeling of depletion if either one is neglected. The fact that the square (90°) aspect in astrology is usually found between two planets in such incompatible elements and the fact that this aspect invariably represents areas of life wherein the person will have to *strive* harder for expression and integration indicates clearly the nature of this dilemma.

However, what is usually not taken into consideration in the interpretation of such aspects or such incompatibilities in traditional astrology is that these combinations represent an interaction of *conscious* and *unconscious* tendencies. This interaction within one person, while it is often productive of severe frustrations and conflicts, can also manifest as specialized skills of a high order. Through the effort to integrate these energies, one will have to develop a high degree of concentration and mastery in the areas indicated; and this can result in the development of a broadened perspective, a deeper understanding, and unusually creative abilities. The following examples should clarify what is meant by this.

Air-Water Combinations

Although this individual often feels pulled between intellectual and emotional orientations to life, this combination at best can produce individuals who are attuned to both realms of experience. Neither the abstract nor the feeling-intuitive world is alien to this person, and he is thus able to develop a mode of operation that encompasses both types of perception. This results in the person being able to give *depth* to his ideas and in his ability to gain *detachment* and *perspective* on his feelings and deeper yearnings. Although this is the most sensitive of all combinations (physically as well as psychologically) and although this sensitivity can prompt one to be a dreamer, escapist, or fantasy-prone malcontent, the sensitivity need not get the better of the person. At best, they have amazingly fertile imaginations, genuinely creative abilities in all the arts and sciences, and specialized skills for dealing with people in all the counseling or healing arts. The ability used in all these fields is that of tuning in on the subtler perceptions of the unconscious and being able to verbalize it concisely.

Air-Earth Combinations

In this combination, although there can be an alternating pull between abstract-conceptual and practical-efficiency orientations, there is not so much conflict as there might seem. This is so since the air and earth signs are ruled by the same planets, thus coloring them with some of the same values, qualities, and modes of operation. One must realize, however, that their compatibility is more evident when found within one individual than when found in two different people's charts in chart comparisons. These elements *are* incompatible energies in their actual mode of expression, but their particular attunements can be considered as complementary. When these energies are focused in some degree of harmony within an individual, he is able to combine intellectual and conceptual awareness with a practical attunement to concrete objectives. He can therefore have a practical grounding upon which his ideas are based and a particularly innovative perspective on getting things done in the material world. This type of person is given to forethought, detachment, practical intelligence, and fairly dry logic. Impulse or emotionalism are not his way of operating, and he often distrusts those who exemplify such qualities. It is an excellent combination for business executives, organizers, or for other types of work that are intellectually demanding. Many people who feel at home in bureaucracies have this combination, for they are able to deal with a wealth of concrete details without getting overwhelmed by the demands on their nervous system.

Water-Fire Combinations

This combination is just the opposite of the preceeding one, for this type expresses everything emotionally, excitedly, and rather impulsively. There is often a lack of logical, systematic thought and procedure, with a resulting restlessness and subjective bias. This is a combination of intensity, emotional extremes, and surprising sensitivity to what others think of them. These people tend to be whole-hoggers, having a marked lack of self-restraint. This lack of control or discipline (which manifests even in people with Scorpio-Leo combinations when they finally let go!) leads in many cases to exceptionally severe swings of mood. These people function in a high-pressure state and, as a rule, they do best when challenged by outer circumstances. Although there can be a conflict between freedom and attachment, between future aspirations and security needs, between ego and selflessness, this combination enables people to moderate their enthusiasm with sensitivity and to express directly their feelings for others. There is usually a simplicity of manner and a refreshingly encouraging quality to these people. At worst, this type is explosively unpredictable, given alternately to inspirations and deep frustrations. At best, they are warm, supportive, and protective in their dealings with others. It is often a good combination for business affairs or for entertainment professions, for they are able to moderate their promotional activities with prudence and to project their feelings with convincing involvement.

Earth-Fire Combinations

This combination has been termed the "steam-roller" by Zipporah Dobyns. She calls it "the most creative and productive of the combinations with the initiative and creativity of fire and the practicality of earth with its urge to produce in tangible form." In her book *Finding the Person in the Horoscope,* Dr. Dobyns further states that this combination "has an impact on the world and is still going when everyone else is dropping by the wayside." This is an accurate description of the interactions of these two elements, for the earth gives sustaining power to the drive for self-expression represented by fire. There is also within these people a practical grounding which they use to test their inspirations, in order to see whether their energy expenditure is potentially productive. These people therefore have the ability to conserve and direct their rather formidable vitality and to channel their enthusiasms toward specific ambitions. The earth attunement gives more patience and discipline to the fire, while the fire provides the confidence and spontaneous faith that earth lacks. These people usually love to work, for they get great satisfaction from seeing the effects of their energies manifested in the world. Many self-motivating entrepreneurs who start small businesses which eventually grow to large enterprises have this combination dominant in their charts.

In the earth-fire combination, there is often a fine balance between egotism and humility, generosity and conservatism. These people are generally happiest when they go off on their own to meet the challenges of the outer world rather than relying on established social roles or educational patterns to attain success. The primary problem of this combination is a certain grossness and insensitivity. "Steam-rollers" are neither reflective about themselves nor particularly careful about whom they crush in their efforts to get where they're going. Hence, they would do well to cultivate more attention to the subtler aspects of life, including their own inner life, ideals, and values. Once this energy is poured into service to others and is directed with full regard to the implications of their actions, the person can actively manifest a powerful love through steadiness, reliability, and productivity.

13

Potential for Integration: Aspects & Planetary Relationships

The emphasized use of the elements in chart interpretation enables the astrological practitioner to understand and explain numerous important factors that might well be ignored if he uses only the major aspects. As a matter of fact, it seems to me that the elements constitute the primary explanation of the aspects, although I by no means underestimate the importance of harmonic theory which is now being given a great deal of attention. As an example, the quincunx (or 150° "inconjunct" aspect) is considered by most astrologers to be a minor aspect indicating some strain involved in the expression of the two planetary principles indicated. This aspect is also related to compulsive and guilt-motivated behavior patterns. If we consider this aspect according to the elements, we find that all quincunxes that involve *inharmonious elements* can indeed be considered as indicative of major life problems, since there is present a constant irritation and annoying compulsiveness that interferes with the easy expression of the planetary principles. (Note: 150° angles can be formed between planets in harmonious elements — e.g., 1° Aries and 29° Leo — but the power of the aspect is thereby weakened.)

Likewise, we have to consider two types of semi-sextiles and semi-squares respectively, if we are to delineate so-called minor aspects with precision. The semi-sextiles and semi-squares are particularly stressful when they involve planets in inharmonious elements. When these aspects are present between two planets in harmonious elements, there is very little stress and indeed the potential for great productivity with relative ease. These same principles of interpretation should be applied to the analysis of squares, trines, and the other aspects as well. A trine, for example, between two planets in inharmonious elements will not signify the same ease of self-expression as trines in the same element, although there will still usually be some definite talent. One might say that the planets' positions according to the elements (without regard to the aspects) reveal the general attunement and tone of energy release in the individual, whereas each close aspect indicates a specific *dynamic* interchange of energy within the person.

One can gain many important revelations about a chart by simply contrasting the different expressions of planetary energies according to the elements, even if there is no aspect involved. This principle is even more important in the comparison of charts, where one is, in effect, analyzing how the energies of two people will interact. The elements, according to Dr. Stone, are like gears that either mesh or grind. Meshing with full harmony can lead to ease of expression and good health, but not necessarily to new insights or to further growth prompted by challenge. The grinding and friction that can develop within a person from the interaction of inharmonious elements inevitably leads to physical strain and psychic tension, but this tension can be productive if creatively expressed. Personal integration may be more difficult in this case, but there is also more likelihood for growth arising out of the need to broaden the dimension of experience represented in order to encompass both factors involved in a certain conflict. In other words, integration of one's seemingly incompatible qualities is possible and indeed potentially creative, for such an inner tension forces one to act and to produce, as well as to grow in awareness of life's complexity. The need to bring together two incompatible elements in one focused outpouring of self-expression can lead to the development of a more complex awareness and indeed of a highly specialized sort of skill, as mentioned in the last chapter.

It is true that the "stressful" aspects, especially the square (90°), between planets inevitably show conflicting or contradictory motives or urges, both simultaneously seeking expression and both interfering with each other. However, the emphasis in traditional astrology on the destructive or self-destructive possibilities of these aspects has prompted many students of astrology to ignore the purpose behind such aspects and the extremely positive results that they can bring. For a well-balanced and reflective presentation of the various aspects, I refer the reader to C.E.O. Carter's *The Astrological Aspects*. This book clearly shows that certain of the trines are commonly indicative of a self-satisfied, apathetic approach to life, and that many of the "stressful" aspects have been found to indicate a potential for greater creativity and higher awareness than is found in the trine between the same two planets.

To sum up what I've been saying relating to the aspects and the four elements: although the aspects are always specifically indicative of special dynamics of energy with which the person will have to contend or upon which he can draw, only the careful comparison of the relative harmony of the elements wherein the Sun, Moon, Ascendant, and other "personal" planets are placed can provide a thorough comprehension of how the person approaches life and what combination of forces he is trying to express.

As an example, a square aspect between the Sun and Moon in inharmonious elements indicates that one tends to "shift gears" in the middle of expressing oneself or receiving from another. This aspect indicates specifically that the subconscious needs (the Moon) inhibit the expression of the more essential conscious desires (the Sun). When one finds this square aspect in inharmonious elements, as is usually the case, there is an obvious inner struggle, manifesting as two prominent personality patterns vying for dominance, an inner conflict which makes others dealing with this person wonder what the individual really means to express. When this square is between the "lights" in harmonious elements, the struggle is not nearly so intense or obvious, although the person will still experience some of the common manifestations of that aspect, such as difficulty in dealing with the opposite sex in close association and the interference of unconscious habit patterns with the easy flow of self-expression.

To further explore the use of the elements in a chart, let us now take the case of a man with the Sun in Virgo and Moon in Leo, having no major or minor aspect between them. The Sun and Moon in this example are in incompatible elements; and, although there will be no conflict or inhibition of the scope indicated by the square aspect mentioned above, there will still be an inner discord and an attempt to express two incompatible modes of being simultaneously. The man's true manner of essential self-expression would be symbolized by Virgo, his Sun sign, and he would be at his best and radiating his most dynamic energy when engaged in Virgoan pursuits and helpful service to others. Humility would suit him well, and his radiance would shine most brightly to others when he was focusing his energies in a Virgo way. However, his Leo moon shows that he has a subconscious need to make a big impression on others, to lord it over the others, and to push himself to the forefront in any activity. One might say that the essential personality of his soul is shown by Virgo, whereas his past conditioning impels him to express himself in a Leo mode, even if it inhibits the solar energy flow. The humility and self-effacing qualities of Virgo do not at all harmonize with the pride and self-aggrandizing habits of Leo, and therefore this combination reflects a major impasse in the path to personal integration even though no aspect is present.

My own experience leads me to believe that one of the first steps in the interpretation of any chart should be to evaluate the relative compatibility of the Sun and Moon, the two primary polarities of the personality as well as the prime indicators of which elements are most highly energized in the individual. An analysis of this depth often leads to insights not accessible to the more common methods of astrological interpretation. Then, as a further step, one can examine the relative compatibility of other pairs of planets: Sun and Mercury; Venus and Mars; Mercury and Jupiter; Jupiter and Saturn; Sun and Venus; Moon and Venus; and so on, in order to define more specifically various modes of self-expression and possible ways of resolving inner conflicts.

A few examples of such a comparison of planetary pairs should clarify what I mean. Take, for example, a man whose Sun is in Sagittarius and Mercury is in Capricorn. His essential nature can be described as Sagittarian: a truth-seeker, open-minded, idealistic, etc. Mercury represents the way in which he approaches new ideas logically and thoughtfully. Since Mercury in Capricorn is known for a particularly sceptical, cautious, and traditional way of thinking, it could reveal that this man's way of thinking could inhibit his *intellectual* acceptance of the very ideals and truths he's so desperately searching for. In that case, even though he would respond to promising new ideas open-mindedly at first hearing, he would eventually have to decide what he valued more: intellectual security and comfort or more essential and deeper needs.

One whose Venus is in an element that is incompatible with that of the Sun likewise could experience a similar inner discord. But in this case, his emotionally-conditioned tastes (Venus) would be in contrast to his more essential needs and values. This can manifest in many ways, for example, tending to attract people into intimate relationships who do not deeply fulfill one's true needs, or trying to express one's affections in a way that does not harmonize with one's higher values.

A similar situation can develop with the Sun and Mars in incompatible elements. For example, take the case of a woman whose Sun is in Aquarius and whose Mars is in Taurus. She would be attracted automatically on a physical level to men who fit the Taurus image, but those same men would simultaneously express themselves at cross-purposes with her more essential Aquarian needs for freedom of self-expression. What is going to give? Will she value the physical attraction over the more essential level of compatibility, or will she come to realize that she can't have everything in one relationship? (Note that a Taurus planet is by sign in square to Aquarius.)

One more example should suffice to explain the procedure I'm getting at. If a man has the Moon in Libra and Venus in Cancer, there are two sets of emotional responses and attunements that are not in harmony. At times he would be attracted to people (especially women) who exemplified the sensitivity and emotional responsiveness of Cancer. With these people, he would feel emotionally free to express his affections and passions, he would feel appreciated, and he would feel a lot of sensual pleasure. However, the Moon represents an even deeper need than does Venus, and so he might in time find that this need was not being satisfied with the Cancer type person. So let us say that he meets a Libra type of woman with whom he feels deeply comfortable and with whom he identifies very strongly. He feels at last that he has met his mate, his "other half", and they marry. Assuming that she does not have much emphasis in water signs to be able to attune to his Venus needs, however, he slowly discovers that a great deal of his emotional life is unfulfilled. And he finds it troublesome that he is slowly beginning to be attracted to the same romantic situations with Cancer types (or at least with watery types) as he was before. He is therefore caught in a bind (Venus square Moon in this case), for his deepest security needs and sense of self and public image (Moon) are all fulfilled by his wife, but his more romantic, sensual and emotional urges (Venus) are frustrated with her. How can he work with both of these needs? How can he fulfill both orientations without ruining his marriage? That is the dilemma, and that is the challenge with which he can work to grow toward greater self-knowledge and emotional refinement.

In this example, the planets are in a traditional aspect (the square), which does tend to bring out a more severe problem. But the basic principles are equally applicable in cases where the Moon and Venus are merely in incompatible elements, without any close aspect. In this procedure of comparing pairs of planets, one is in effect analyzing two specific attunements which may inhibit the expression of each other's fundamental principles. It is as if the two planets get in each other's way, but yet the individual will invariably have to fulfill both needs and express both urges if he is to feel that he's living a full life. This doesn't mean that the individual *will succeed* in his attempts to resolve the dilemma, but merely that the attempt to do so is a major life challenge through which he can broaden his understanding of himself and of life in general. As Jung states, a true conflict is never resolvable on the same level of consciousness where it is experienced. It can only be outgrown. When the individual has grown in awareness to the point where both sides of a conflict are seen and accepted, the experience of conflict can begin to dissolve.

14

Planets in the Elements

In order to attain the in-depth level of chart interpretation just described, one naturally has to have a way of expressing the attunement of each planet in the chart in a concise and practical way. The interpretation of all the planets is made more useful and more specifically accurate by an understanding of the elements involved, for the planets in the elements show not only how we are attuned to different dimensions of experience but also how we can consciously *tune in* to these dimensions and with what energies we contact these fields of life activity in an immediate way. The planets represent specific principles of energy exchange between the individual and the universal supply of all energy. Each planet therefore reveals not only a type of *outgoing* energy and an urge toward *expression* of a certain kind, but also it reveals a specific *need* for activity and fulfillment that must be fed along a particular *incoming* wavelength.

(See the Key Concepts for the Planets at the end of Chapter 9.)

Mercury

As an example, Mercury represents not only an urge to express one's thoughts to others and to establish one's thoughts specifically through verbal expression or manual skill, but it also shows the need to be understood by another person who is attuned to ideas in a similar way and the need to learn by receiving ideas and information from the outer world. In other words, Mercury symbolizes the urge to establish contact and true give-and-take communication with others; and the mode of energy exchange represented is the inflow (through perception) and the outflow (through skill, speech, and manual dexterity) of intelligence. The element wherein Mercury is found in a particular chart indicates what specific energy and quality influences one's "logic" and how one thinks and expresses thoughts along a certain vibratory wavelength. Mercury in water signs, for example, indicates a mode of communication strongly influenced by one's deepest *yearnings* and sub-conscious predispositions. Mercury in the earth signs shows that one's thoughts are influenced by practical *needs* and by the individual's preference to accept ideas that are applicable in a practical way. Mercury in the air signs reveals that one's thoughts are relatively free and unfettered by emotional and practical needs and that they can therefore be as abstract as the person wants. In other words, since the key word for the air element is *concepts,* Mercury is very much at home in the air signs, for the intellectual mind can function with a degree of relative freedom and lightness. Mercury in the fire signs indicates that one's thoughts are influenced by one's *aspirations,* beliefs, hopes, and personal plans. Mercury in the fire signs does not therefore represent the same objectivity of thought found in the air signs, but it does often signify a definite and purposeful use of positive thinking.

This attunement of Mercury about which we have been speaking is especially evident when one studies chart comparisons and realizes that the specific words spoken in any attempt at communication are not nearly so important as the energy behind those words. For example, if you are attuned to another person through harmonious aspects between each person's Mercury, you will be able to tune in on his or her thoughts even if they are poorly expressed. On the other hand, if your Mercury is in conflict with, or at least not attuned to, that of another person, you'll most likely have difficulty "hearing" what the person is saying even if the individual is highly articulate. This vibration of Mercury is evident to some extent even in written communication, but it is especially obvious in person-to-person contacts.

As an example, a woman in one of my astrology classes (who was sitting way in the back of the room about twenty rows from the front) one night asked a question about some topic being discussed. Before she was through verbalizing the question, I noticed that I had already understood her completely with an unusual degree of clarity. I asked her what sign her Mercury was

in, and she replied that it was in the same sign as mine and very
nearly the same degree! That immediately explained to me why I
had so completely and quickly understood her question; for, not
only had I comprehended the words she was using to pose the
question, but I had also automatically tuned in on her consciousness and so had simultaneously understood all the nuances
motivating her query. In other cases, during the course of classes
I've taught, I have noticed the opposite thing happening at times:
a person to whom I am not at all attuned trying rather desperately to phrase a question in a way I can understand. In such
cases, I have to use extra mental energy to, in effect, change my
natural attunement to the other person's in order to be capable of
understanding thoughts expressed in a rather foreign vibration.

This conscious re-attunement or change of phase — necessary
at times to attune to another person — is something that one can
to some extent also do with the energies of other planets. For
example, if you find that the way you express affection (Venus)
puts off another person whom you want to please, it is possible to
moderate the expression of your own Venus energy and to tune in
on what exactly will be pleasing to the other person. There is,
however, an immediate and automatic reticence to change levels
of expression, for to do so requires the use of extra energy in order
to work in a foreign realm of experience. One can do so through
conscious effort and concentration, but it is inevitably wearing on
the person if he or she attempts to express self over some period of
time in a way that does not flow naturally. This fact is especially
relevant to the consideration of certain kinds of incompatibility in
chart comparisons, which we will explore in the next chapter.

Before considering the other planets, we should make it clear at
this point that the relative importance and intensity of the various planets' elements are to be considered in depth before one
makes any statement about the strength of elements in a certain
chart or about a specific type of incompatibility in a chart comparison. It is much easier to periodically modify the attunement
or expression of Mercury, Venus, Mars, or Jupiter than it is to
attempt to do so with the Sun, Moon, or Ascendant. In fact, since
the Sun-Moon polarity and the Ascendant combine to vitalize
one's entire being, these energies cannot really be modified sub-

stantially in any healthy way; they can only be blocked or repressed. This is so because the Sun, Moon, and Ascendant show what energies (according to their elements) dominate your attention consistently, whereas the elements of Mercury, Venus, Mars, and Jupiter function more periodically and in rather specific situations.

Venus

Like Mercury, the planet Venus represents an inflow and outflow of energy, and its placement in the various elements is expressed as the give and take of love, affection, sensual pleasure, and caring with others. The element of one's Venus represents how one expresses appreciation and caring, in other words how one gives of one's own feelings. That is the outflowing phase of the Venus principle in action, but the inflowing phase is equally important. It represents, according to the element of its sign position, what sorts of experience and types of expression feed one's need for closeness with another and help one to feel loved and appreciated. If one's Venus is in a water sign, for example, there is the need for a constant emotional feeding and sympathetic caring, and for a consistent and steady responsiveness to one's sensitivity and vulnerability. This sort of sharing requires no words (one of the chief means of expression for Venus in the air signs), no grand gestures (like Venus in the fire signs), and no tangible commitments (like Venus in the earth signs.) Venus in water signs requires only an interchange of sensitivity and love feelings which may easily go unnoticed by others who are not attuned similarly.

Mars

The element of Mars shows what types of experiences and modes of activity stimulate one's physical energy and with what energy one seeks to assert oneself. For example, those with Mars in air signs try to assert themselves through the expression of ideas, whereas Mars in fire signs operates through more direct physical action. Mars in water signs functions more subtly, harnessing emotional power in some cases and asserting self toward desires that are not fully conscious in other cases. Mars in the earth signs indicates that the person needs to express his will and assertive power through concrete achievement which requires patience and persistence.

Another way of phrasing the type of energy exchange which Mars represents is that the element of one's Mars is the energy that feeds your need for physical excitement and the mode through which you can express your aggressive powers to prove your strength. It describes the specific method you use to get what you want: Mars in air uses persuasion, Mars in fire uses power and initiative, Mars in earth uses patience and efficiency, and Mars in water use slyness, intuition, and a rather unconquerable persistence. A brother of mine, for example, puts most of his energy into raising plants from seed, some of which require several years of growth before they'll be ready for market. The patience and nurturing quality needed for this type of work is well represented by his Mars in Taurus, and it is an example of Mars energy being utilized in a way which harmonizes with its true attunement.

Sun, Moon, & Ascendant

The Sun sign element has been discussed rather thoroughly in earlier chapters, and therefore there is no need to deal with it further in any detail here. One can simply say that the element of the Sun is the energy which feeds one's basic sense of purpose and feeling of well-being. The element of the Ascendant is somewhat similar, although it denotes a way of approaching life that is more specific and less all-encompassing than the Sun's element. The element of the Ascendant reveals the mode of expression of one's entire self *in action* in the world, a natural and spontaneous way of immediately confronting life outside one's self. It reveals what sort of approach to outer life one would prefer to take in order to feel free and unencumbered by other concerns, but there are often other factors in the chart which can inhibit such an intensely personalized approach (especially close aspects to the Ascendant). One can say, however, that the element of the Ascendant represents a type of self-projection that is physically energizing and which has a strong impact on one's self-confidence and sense of individual freedom and uniqueness.

The element of the Moon's position represents an attunement from the past that manifests automatically, a mode of feeling and being that one needs to pay attention to in order to feel inwardly secure and at home with one's self. This element and experiences related to it feed your need to feel *right* about yourself; for, by such modes of self-expression, you are satisfying a deep inner need that can give stability to your entire personality. The Moon's element also shows how you react instinctively to all experiences, with what energy you adjust yourself to the flow of life spontaneously.

For example, if the Moon is in an air sign, one will have to express one's thoughts to others in order to feel right about oneself and in order to feel an inner peace and tranquility coming from the satisfaction of that subconscious need. Likewise, one will adjust oneself to life by first gaining detachment on any experience in an effort to evaluate objectively whatever is at hand. In other words, one with the Moon in an air sign always reacts by thinking first, and then acting according to the dictates of his evaluation. This quality of forethought is usually quite absent in people who have the Moon in water or fire signs, although it is present in those whose Moon is in earth signs.

The Moon in water signs indicates a way of reacting colored by emotional intensity. This can manifest as fear or feeling vulnerable, or it can simply indicate an immediate and deep involvement with every demand placed upon the person by life. The person will inevitably have to contend with past conditioning and old habit patterns as a daily requirement in his efforts to adjust to changing circumstances within and without.

The Moon in fire signs is found in the charts of people who react to changing conditions or to immediate circumstances with enthusiasm and direct action. They tend to leap before they look, but they are never known for lack of decisiveness. Impatience is often a problem, however, especially when the Moon is in Aries or Sagittarius.

The Moon in the earth signs indicates one who tends to react in a very grounded, steady, matter-of-fact way. The reaction is so self-contained in those with Taurus or Capricorn Moon, in fact, that others often think there is no reaction at all! Those with Moon in Virgo, however, generally react quite obviously and nervously to any stimulus. It might be mentioned here that those with the Moon in Virgo or Capricorn have a hard time feeling *right* about themselves; self-acceptance for these people is generally based on the amount and quality of practical work accomplished, and their ability to adjust to life successfully usually depends upon their role in the world of work. It is in this area of life that those with the Moon in the "work" signs feel *at home*.

Jupiter & Saturn

Jupiter's element shows what sorts of experiences and modes of activity generate an inner faith and confidence in oneself. To state this another way, one is able to experience a protective feeling of unity with a greater power or plan when one operates on the level indicated by Jupiter's element. Saturn's element, on the other hand, indicates at what level of expression one tends to be inhibited and where one's energy is blocked or restricted. This inner blockage arises because that level of experience is *overly-*important to the individual. He therefore tends to tie himself up in knots in this area of life and to constrict the flow of this energy by either *trying too hard* to express it or by avoiding or repressing it. This over-emphasis often leads to a state of fear and anxiety related to the sort of experience indicated, until one has learned to relax, let go, and to tune in on the trust and faith symbolized by Jupiter. Saturn and Jupiter may be interpreted usefully as a pair of complementary principles: Saturn represents effort, Jupiter represents grace. Effort without grace leaves one no joy or serenity, nor is one then able to accept the benefits of his effort. Grace without effort is generally not a constructive way to go through life; for, although one may have great faith and optimism, there is usually very little that gets done and the reliance on grace alone can become a hollow escape from immediate duties.

The element of Saturn in one's chart generally indicates (especially if the aspects to Saturn are stressful) a specific problem with fully accepting, without fear, that level of experience represented by the particular element. This fear is often an outgrowth of an old pattern of life that has now become intolerably rigid and oppressive, although at one time (such as in past lives) this caution and self-discipline could have served a useful purpose. Indeed, the caution and discipline may still serve a highly useful purpose in one's growth, but only if it is accepted as a challenge motivating one to make a more *consistent* effort to express oneself concretely in that area of life. Effort is necessary to open the channel so that the energy can flow naturally, but rigidly forcing the flow is as self-defeating as blocking it altogether.

For example, Saturn in a water sign often indicates a fear of emotional expression. Some authors have stated that such a position of Saturn makes one cold and unfeeling, but the reality is just the opposite. Those with Saturn in a water sign are *overly*-sensitive emotionally, for they are too rigidly involved with defending their sensitive feelings from the threats of the outer world. They naturally, therefore, tend to be extremely cautious about expressing their feelings openly, for that would make them vulnerable. Saturn in water signs can indicate a severe degree of emotional repression, but that still does not mean that the person isn't feeling anything! People with this position of Saturn in their charts need to make a concentrated effort to express their feelings with discipline, focus, and self-acceptance. As long as one is tied up in knots, he will continue to over-react to anything, in the same way as a nervous fearful person will jump at the slightest noise. But when the individual has learned to unwind, to let go, and to accept himself, he is then able to direct consciously all the energy that previously was blocked up by fears and negative attitudes.

One often finds that people will express the element of Saturn's position in their work, for this is a way of giving definite focus to these energies in a concrete way. Those with Saturn in the water signs therefore are often attracted to types of work in which they can express their emotions and sensitivity to others, for example in the healing arts or in dealing with those who are suffering in other ways. Through their work, they can establish an emotional strength that is unshakable, and it can then be a real asset to the person's character rather than remaining a crippling liability. Likewise, we can briefly mention Saturn in the other elements. Saturn in the air signs indicates the need to stabilize one's *understanding,* and these people will often express their sensitivity to other people as well as their knowledge in their daily work. Saturn in the fire signs shows the need to stabilize one's *identity*, and people with this placement of Saturn often find that their real work is to create new forms for their self-expression, whether in the arts or in business. Those with Saturn in earth signs need to stabilize their *efficiency* and it is important to them to express reliability and precision in their daily work.

Whereas the element of Saturn in any birth-chart indicates a type of energy that is naturally rather restricted (at least in youth), Jupiter's element symbolizes a reservoir of vitality that is abundant and naturally flowing. As an example of the difference between these two planets' functions, let us consider each of them in the sign Leo. Jupiter in Leo indicates that a dramatic, fiery, rather flamboyant mode of self-expression would be needed to give one a sense of inner faith and confidence. Likewise, Saturn in Leo also indicates one who at least subconsciously wants to express himself in this way; but the desire is usually too rigidly self-centered, too involved with one's ego-identity, thus creating a fear of failure or vulnerability that can cripple one's self-confidence. Because of this fear, one tends to restrict oneself or to overly-discipline oneself in this area, an effort that aggravates an already vicious circle of inner frustration. If, on the other hand, the individual will accept the fact that he or she desperately needs to *express* that energy, no matter what effort it requires, the first step toward getting the energy flowing will have been taken. But this step is impossible without realizing that the need so strongly felt is a manifestation of life's need to express itself rather than simply a personal "hang-up." Saturn's element shows where one needs to develop trust in a greater power than mere ego. Both Jupiter and Saturn in a particular element indicate a great need for expression in that particular mode, but the quality of energy release is very different. Jupiter's element tends to flow rather spontaneously (if it is not blocked by Saturn!) and even excessively, whereas Saturn's element is expressed through conscientious effort and patient work at self-disciplined action.

Other Considerations

In interpreting the various planets in the elements, one has to have a rather deep understanding of the specific functional principle represented by a planet in order to utilize these insights to the fullest extent. Once this understanding has been achieved through years of study and patient practice on hundreds of charts, many of the ancient astrological ideas come alive with heightened significance. For example, the concepts of exaltation, dignity, fall and detriment, rather than being merely outmoded remnants of an archaic system as has been stated by some modern writers, are then seen to have highly practical meaning. Although such a classification of planetary positions is essentially based upon the harmony between a particular planet's nature and the quality of a certain element, and although any planet in a certain element does indicate certain general qualities of expression, it is necessary to consider each *sign* placement of a planet individually in order to understand fully the meaning of such concepts.

For example, if a planet is in a sign that is somewhat incompatible with its own nature, it is as if *the quality of that sign "interferes" with the pure expression of that principle.* If a person has, for instance, Mercury in Sagittarius, there is a tendency for his beliefs and aspirations (Sagittarius) to interfere with the expression of his logic and rational thought (Mercury). This does not mean that the individual is necessarily lacking in intelligence or clear perception, but rather it signifies that his ideas are invariably colored by concerns other than pure reason and factual analysis. Such a person, when asked to explain why he just made a certain statement, will most likely refer to the belief, ideal, or hope that motivated his statement rather than giving his listener specific facts to support the idea. It can be seen that Mercury's "detriment" in Sagittarius, therefore, does not indicate something "bad" about the person or something which is necessarily a liability (as detriments are often interpreted), but rather it indicates a specific personal difficulty in expressing the true nature of that planet's functional principle. The degree of difficulty experienced will be dependent upon the aspects to that planet and upon the individual's level of awareness.

One other example should suffice to point the reader in the direction of utilizing these ancient principles constructively. Supposing one has Venus in Scorpio (another "detriment"), the demands, insatiable emotional needs, and intense desires of Scorpio tend to interfere with the expression of affection and with the *free* exchange of love feelings with another person. This is not to say that such an individual cannot express affection or love; it merely points to the fact that such a person will experience within himself or herself a certain degree of emotional turmoil resulting from the realization that true love feelings are continually being colored by passion, sexual desires, and emotional demands. What the person will *do* about this state of affairs is not indicated in the birth-chart, for the same energy can manifest in many ways. (See the Positive-Negative Expression of Planetary Principles at the end of Chapter 9.) The placement of the planets in certain signs inevitably reveals certain urges and needs, although how aware the person is of these inner dynamics cannot be determined solely through the chart. How easily the particular urge or need can be expressed and fulfilled is indicated by the aspects to that planet, and it is the more stressful aspects that generally indicate a certain build-up or blockage of a certain element's expression.

15

Elements in Chart Comparison

The elements are the key to a full understanding of the art of synastry, commonly called "chart comparisons." In comparing any two charts, even more so than in work with individual charts, one must take into consideration the relative harmony of the positions of the planets according to the elements as well as analyzing the specific aspects between one person's planets and those of the other person. As mentioned earlier, the closest aspects indicate a more dynamic interchange of energy than is indicated by the elements alone, but a thorough analysis of the harmony of two people's planets according to the elements will enable the practiced astrologer to discover many important insights and subtle differentiations that the closest aspects themselves do not fully elucidate.

On the level of normal experience, any relationship may be viewed as an interaction of two energy fields. Although many refinements may be brought into play, the art of comparing charts is essentially an analysis of how the energies of two people exchange with one another. This is not to say that there is no deeper meaning behind this apparent play of energies, such as past life karma. But, as far as most astrologers are reliably able to perceive, this relative compatibility of energies is the fact at hand with which they have to deal. An analysis of the harmony of elements in a chart comparison reveals how and where the two people are able to *feed* each other's energy field, as well as how the two block each other's energy flow and therefore frustrate each other. When a blockage exists, there is an experience of either great frustration or severe depletion of energy, or sometimes both. When there is a mutual harmonious interchange of energy, there is an experience of satisfaction, vitalization, and completeness. Naturally, in most relationships, there will be both types of energy exchange; but the overall emphasis will usually predominate. The harmonious exchanges between two people will provide resources upon which both people may draw in order to provide the necessary energy required to deal with other areas of the relationship that are more problematical. If, however, there is a predominance of stressful and discordant energy exchange between two people, it is only a matter of time until one or both desire to end the relationship out of sheer exhaustion if nothing else.

I have been mentioning how people "feed" each other's energy fields, and — in order to clarify what I mean by this — let us refer here to a quotation from the book *Born to Heal*. The healer Mr. A, whom we mentioned earlier, emphasizes the element of the Sun sign as one of the most important features of any relationship being studied:

> "There are compatible, neutral, and negative types of energy. Compatible, or matching, energies together generate revitalizing energy for magnetic fuel."

Compatible energies are considered by Mr. A to be those of the same element but of different signs. The "negative" energies are the incompatible elements, such as water and fire. Their "combined action causes a depletion of the magnetic field at different levels, thereby losing its drawing power on human energy taken in by the lungs." Neutral energies are considered by Mr. A to be those of the same Sun sign who don't have other compatible energies to refuel them. They ordinarily do not refuel each other effectively, and they tend to blend and "act as one element." Hence, those with the Sun in the same sign who don't have other compatible, energizing attunements often find that a slow starvation of the nervous system can result. It is not necessarily that they are in conflict with each other, but simply that neither person is easily "fed" a slightly different and enlivening vibration of that same element. The combination of other "harmonious" elements such as air and fire, or water and earth, is considered to be less compatible than the different signs of the same element, but much more compatible than Mr. A's "negative" energies.

Mr. A goes on to say that our nervous system, through our magnetic field, is influenced by every person with whom we come in contact: "If one's own generation of energy is strong, these cross energies from others have little or no effect on our nerves. If we are weakened or depleted, however, reaction is likely." He also points out that a child will automatically gravitate to the parent who feeds his magnetic field. If both parents' energies are discordant with his energy pattern, the result is often a child who is delicate and high-strung, his nature being a mystery to the parents. I have many time noticed this phenomenon in my practice. One example that come to mind is a girl whose parents are Cancer and Taurus Sun signs. She herself is a Leo with Moon in Aries. During her adolescence particularly, she was considered to be a problem child by her parents, and she was extremely nervous and insecure for someone with so much fiery energy. A great change took place in her within two years of her leaving home after high school, and — needless to say — she left home as soon as she could after graduation. Once on her own and no longer having to contend daily with the cross-currents of her parents' energies, she quickly developed the poise and confidence that one would normally associate with a person of her attunement. In other words, *she* was not the problem; the *relationship* between her and the parents was the problem. And what psychologist without the help of astrology could have figured out this dilemma?

Although the Sun's element is the primary fuel of the individual, the elements of the Moon and Ascendant are inevitably highly energized in any person. And, as has been explained at length, the elements of the other personal planets and particularly of the Sun's and Ascendant's "rulers" must be taken into consideration in any chart comparison. Everyone is attuned to some extent with all the elements, but the most dynamic and conscious attunement is indicated by the major factors in the birth-chart just mentioned. Particularly the elements of the Sun-Moon polarity are highly energized, and the individual therefore will be most harmonious and responsive with another person who shares some of that same attunement. Although there are many cases of a marriage, for example, wherein the man's Sun and Moon elements are incompatible with the woman's Sun and Moon elements, the vast majority of those marriages either don't last long or endure in spite of one or both people's constant frustration. I am not proposing that every type of relationship necessarily has to have a harmonious relationship between each person's Sun and Moon elements (for, as stated above, there are other factors to consider), but I am emphasizing that the most harmonious and all-encompassing compatibility is impossible without some similar smooth interchange of energy. This is so because the harmony between the Sun, for example, and another person's Sun or Moon is indicative of the purest expression and most immediate blending of the two peoples' vital energies.

The relative importance of such an aspect depends, of course, on the type of relationship being analyzed, the degree of intimacy involved, the closeness of the association, and the amount of time the two spend in each other's company. A distant business relationship would not test the compatibility so deeply as a relationship involving marriage partners or parent and child. The harmony between Suns and Moons is indicative of a mutual identification with the other, an immediate awareness of the two people's oneness. There is in such cases a blending of identity, a mutual vitalization, and a natural encouragement of each person's essential self-expression. This type of rapport, in other words, is indicative of one of the highest forms of love, a type of mutual acceptance and responsiveness that is far more lasting and more deeply satisfying than relationships based purely upon harmonious Venus-Venus, Venus-Mars, Venus-Sun, or Venus-Moon aspects.

As an example of what I'm emphasizing here, let us examine the case of a married couple. The woman has Sun in Leo and Moon in Aries, Venus in Virgo, Mars in Taurus, and Cancer Rising. (This is a different woman than the Leo with Aries Moon mentioned earlier in this chapter.) Her ex-husband has Sun in Capricorn, Moon in Virgo, Mars in Gemini, Venus in Sagittarius, and Cancer rising. Since this is not a book devoted primarily to chart comparisons, I am not going to analyze all aspects of the comparison. But I do want to point out a few critical factors to elucidate the importance of the elements in comparisons. Both people have Cancer rising, and both have shared raising two children for twelve years. The emphasis on home and family has naturally been an important focus of energy for each of them, and indeed this similar orientation helped them to keep the marriage going as long as they did (twelve years). Both people are therefore ruled by the Moon, but their Moons are in incompatible elements. Neither of their Suns or Moons is in harmony with the other's Sun or Moon. The woman's chief element is fire, and the man's is earth. They live in different worlds; they function in totally different and inharmonious ways; different things are important to them; what is *real* to one is not at all important to the other. Neither the woman's Venus nor Mars is harmonious with the man's Venus and Mars, and — as she admitted — she had totally ceased to respond to her husband sexually years ago.

Now what brought these people together, astrologically speaking? What ever made them feel that they were compatible, that they could indeed make each other happy? The woman's Venus in Virgo is closely conjunct his Moon and trine his Sun. Her Mars is trine his Sun and Moon. Hence, his essential Sun-Moon energy activated her romantic, sexual, and love energies at first meeting. His earthiness is quite compatible with her own earthiness and particularly with her attraction to earthy men on a physical level (Mars in Taurus). But his earthiness is not compatible with her *essential* fiery nature! Likewise, his Venus in Sagittarius is trine her Sun and Moon, and his Mars is sextile each light. Again, her essential Sun-Moon vitality activated his emotional and sexual energies. Her fiery energy is very compatible with his fire sign Venus (attraction to fiery women) and harmonious with his air sign Mars. But, as an essentially earthy type of person, he may get a kick out of her fire, but he can't really tune in on her way of being. In the course of doing chart comparisons for many married people or lovers, this seems to be the most common of all factors contributing to a slow dissolution of the relationship: whereas the people like each other in many ways and indeed are often very emotionally and sexually stimulated by each other, one or both people slowly realize that they simply can't be themselves fully in the relationship, that — not matter how hard they work at it — they cannot share their innermost self with the other

This is so because, if one is not attuned strongly to a certain element, it is virtually impossible to participate fully in that realm of being and that quality of consciousness. Two such people will therefore find themselves increasingly distant from each other, as the two grow, evolve, and individualize in their different ways. The more they grow in awareness of their essential individuality, the more they will become resigned to the fact that they will never be able to share at the level of depth that they might want. The degree of dissatisfaction depends of course upon each person's expectations in the relationship, how dependent on the relationship each is for self-fulfillment, and what degree of *personal* intensity is sought through the involvement. A very impersonal Capricorn, for example, may be satisfied with a marriage (simply because its basic structure is secure and comfortable) that would be ultimately frustrating for a Libra.

It seems to me that one of the reasons for the Western world's increasing divorce statistics is that more and more people are becoming aware of their individuality and more and more insistent on expressing it. This trend has simply been speeded up by the transit of Uranus through Libra. The pace of life, the breakdown of traditional values, the rootlessness of most American families have all contributed to this pattern; but there is a positive side to this social trend which is often ignored: more people are focusing upon the importance of a conscious and fulfilling relationship with others than in previous decades. The new and increasing emphasis upon personal liberty and individuality has naturally manifested in some extreme ways since people always tend to go to extremes when they break away from traditions or restrictive life-styles. However, once this new freedom (greatly heightened as the age of Aquarius comes into full play) is accepted and integrated with spiritual values, it is my feeling that the upheavals now being experienced in relationship structures will calm down. In fact, Pluto transiting through Libra might well put the finishing touches on the revolution that Uranus activated, and we might find before too many years that the entire structure of marriage and close relationships has been reborn at a new and more conscious level.

In doing chart comparisons, it should be noted with particular emphasis that one should not take the astrological data as an absolutely determining indication of the "misery" or "happiness" to be experienced in a certain relationship. The proper use of astrological information is to further the depth of understanding in order that individuals may live more consciously, not to provide excuses for the evasion of responsibilities or to foster illusions of ultimate bliss. The level of awareness of the two people involved is always the most important factor, and the way they choose to deal with what may be conflicting tendencies or personality patterns is predictable only to the degree that the people function unconsciously. If the individuals are highly aware people and/or have certain spiritual or ethical ideals that they both are trying to incorporate into their lives, they may be able to deal constructively with obstacles that would destroy a relationship between less aware people.

People are often attracted to others who are attuned to an element that they themselves lack. A number of writers on the subject of chart comparisons have stated that such a situation is ideal since the people "complement" one another, each providing something that the other needs. This is one of the many astrological statements that sounds great on paper but often doesn't work in practice. It is a fact that we are often intrigued by and attracted to others who exemplify qualities or abilities that we aren't endowed with. However, my experience indicates that it is only rarely that we can deal with such a person *intimately* over a long period of time with any degree of contentment. This type of relationship is more likely to be satisfactory if it is seen as a fairly short-term growth-oriented arrangement rather than as a long term contract in marriage or business. Some writers have even gone so far as to assert that the ideal relationship exemplifies a perfect balance of the elements between the two people, with one providing, for example, the fire and earth while the other's attunement is water and air. Again, this sounds better in theory than it works in experience, for two such people will often be so different that the gap between their consciousness and experience will grow wider with every year. They usually find that they are increasingly unable to participate in each other's worlds.

There are naturally exceptions to most rules, and the practicing astrologer will occasionally come across a relationship that seems to be successful even though the two people are not attuned to each other very strongly by the elements. But in these cases, there is inevitably some powerful contact between the two charts that has motivated both people to work it out. For, although the elemental attunement is of major importance in comparisons, the specific aspects between charts must be considered systematically and in great detail in any thorough examination of a specific relationship. Some of the chart comparison methods proposed in various articles and books are quite radical over-simplifications of this highly complex art, and the astrologer who relies upon such half-way methods cannot hope to understand relationships in any depth. I am not emphasizing the elements' importance to the exclusion of the more traditional methods of analyzing inter-chart aspects, but I am simply trying to elucidate the deeper foundations of what is happening in any relationship on the energy level. For instance, although close aspects in a chart comparison will always indicate a specific type of energy flow or blockage, two people who are harmoniously attuned according to the elements have a much better chance of constructively meeting the challenges of their stressful aspects.

Even if we are involved in a relationship with someone whose dominant element is one that we lack, we can learn a great deal from that person. When we have grown aware of our own incapacities and needs for future growth, we can at the very least more fully appreciate the qualities of such people and admire them for their ability to express themselves in a realm that is foreign to us. This may require a certain detachment in the relationship, but it by no means always indicates that the relationship is devoid of fulfillment and deep satisfaction.

From the foregoing, we can conclude that having the Sun, for example, in the same sign (or even in the same element) as another person's Moon is an important and harmonious contact between any two people regardless of whether there exists a close aspect between the two lights. Likewise, although Mars-Venus trines are traditionally considered to be particularly harmonious aspects for love and sexuality, having Mars in a trine to another's Venus is not indicative of particular compatibility *if* the planets are in incompatible elements. For a penetrating and accurate interpretation of specific aspects in chart comparisons, I urge the reader to study Lois H. Sargent's *How to Handle Your Human Relations* (published by American Federation of Astrologers).

Since most of the principles involved in comparing the interaction and combination of elements have already been dealt with in this book, there is not need to repeat them here. (Chapter 10 contains some material on how people of each element tend to react toward those of different attunement.) It would be useful, however, in order to get a feeling of how these energies combine, for the reader to visualize the physical manifestations of the elements as they interact with each other. What does water do when it meets earth? What does air do when it meets water? What is the interaction between these elements? Once one has assimilated the essential nature of an element, it is relatively a simple matter to understand its interaction with the others. Not only does such a visualization contribute to a deeper understanding of the psychological dynamics involved, but it is also useful for gaining insight into how people effect each other's health simply by their being together.

It is quite common in practice to come across cases in which a man and woman, although they might like each other a great deal, find that they are consistently devitalized by spending too much time together. In other cases, the interaction of two people's energy fields is so intensely vitalizing that one or both people find that they can't tolerate that level of intensity. It is as if they were being over-amped electrically, thus short-circuiting their nervous systems and blowing fuses repeatedly. Both types of relationships can only be understood in terms of the elements. For example, if a Cancer lives with a Gemini, the Cancer might feel "dried out," evaporated, lifeless. The Gemini may feel smothered, have a hard time getting out of bed in the morning, and may even develop breathing difficulties. It is as if the Gemini were trying to live "under water" and the Cancer were trying to live stranded up in the air. Both people's energy fields could become quite devitalized, and they may be surprised at how relieved and how energized they feel when they move apart.

In the other type of case, assume that a Sagittarius with Moon in Leo was living with a Gemini with Moon in Aquarius. Now this could be a positive and harmonious relationship *if* both people could stand the level of intensity. The rest of the comparison would tell that. But, since each person's Sun and Moon is opposite the other's (and many oppositions, rather than being frustrating or blocking in chart comparisons, indicate tremendous *stimulation* of energy flow), the level of intensity might be so great that neither person can operate effectively when within range of the other person's magnetic power. They would feel drawn together (absolutely polarized along the Sun and Moon wavelengths), but they may also feel the need to pull apart in order to maintain their own energy integrity and functional capacity.

Many living-together situations are improved and the health of one or both people takes an upturn if the two people sleep in different bedrooms. This is an especially useful change to make if the two are of radically different attunement. It is not a very romantic thing to do, but it is beneficial in many relationships. The reason for this is that, if two people are sleeping in the same room (and especially if they are in the same bed), their energy fields are constantly interacting throughout the night, either vitalizing each other or depleting the other's energy reservoir. Merging one's energy with another's for eight consecutive hours has a dramatically powerful influence on each person's state of health, for good or ill; and it seems rather foolish to persist in such a habit simply for the sake of satisfying romantic images in the mind if the effect of it is the dissipation of one's vitality. I personally know many people who have complained of the devitalizing effects of sleeping with their partner and whose energy picked up markedly when they slept in different rooms. On the other hand, I have also known cases where the people vitalize each other so much during the night that they each need no more than six hours sleep and are always in splendid health.

The effect on an individual's health of being in close proximity with another has been underestimated and usually ignored by the medical and psychological professions. But the fact remains that, in the presence of another who has a particularly strong energy field, we are affected more than we may realize, even if the other person isn't in the same room but is merely living in the same house. A friend of mine whose Sun is in Pisces and whose ascendant is Scorpio (both very sensitive water signs!) was once assigned to share an office with a Scorpio Sun man. Any student of astrology knows that the magnetic field of a Scorpio person is usually of overpowering strength and that such a person's presence cannot be ignored. My friend found that he could not get any work done so long as the Scorpio was in the room. He finally arranged to work evenings and weekends when he would be the only person in the office. This type of experience cannot be "explained away" as paranoia, over-sensitivity, or projection as many psychologists would attempt to do. It is an experience based on a real interaction of two people's energy fields, the level of activity at the basis of all psychological and physical manifestations.

In order to be truly healthy (the words "healthy" and "heal" derive from an Old English word meaning *whole*), one must be nourished at all levels. One must feed all four elements or bodies: the emotional, mental, physical, and spiritual. Any aspect of one's nature that is not sufficiently fed soon begins to atrophy. Just as a hungry person soon gets desperate and will do almost anything for food, so any aspect of man's fourfold nature begins to rebel and to demand feeding and attention if it is being neglected. A well-balanced life is one in which the individual pays due attention to all his primary needs; and the attunement represented in the birth-chart reveals how one is imbalanced, what needs are being neglected (lack of an element), what dimensions of life are being over-emphasized (too much of one element), and what aspects of the nature are in need of refinement or transformation (particularly the stressfully aspected planets in a certain element).

I do not mean to give the impression that an unthinking insistence upon fulfilling every urge is the answer to all problems and the key to good health. The degree of refinement of our energy nourishment is important. As one grows in consciousness, one is able to be satisfied with a more refined and subtle type of feeding. Through experience, one can learn to tune in on his essential energy requirements and to satisfy them in simple and direct ways with full awareness of what he is doing and why. For example, everyone needs some quantity of material nourishment, but most people eat much more than they need, much poorer quality food than the body requires for proper nutrition, and they often eat in such a state of hurry and excitement that the food is not properly assimilated. Paying some attention to the body's real nutritional requirements and to how the process of digestion and assimilation operates can enable one to sustain the physical body healthfully on a simple, pure, and economical diet.

Likewise, everyone needs some emotional input on a regular basis. But how are these emotional needs really satisfied? The more refined and concentrated the emotional experience is, the more deeply nourishing it is for the inner being. Simply allowing the emotional needs to dictate our behavior compulsively is a sure way to waste energy, to disrupt one's life-structure, and ultimately to experience emotional starvation. Modern civilization is structured in such a way that it ensures a complete starvation of man's most essential needs, and that constant state of energy deprivation is no doubt a primary cause of the desperate and hysterical behavior we so often witness. In urban civilization, if one fully participates in the cultural patterns of life-style, work, and dietary habits, he finds himself utterly without physical, emotional, mental and spiritual substance to maintain himself in a state of wholeness. The times today dictate that each person take responsibility for his own needs, and a knowledge of the four elements and their functions is a personal education in the operative principles of life's essential forces.

NOTE: More detailed explanations of other factors to be considered in chart comparisons can be found in the following works by the author: Chapter 7 ("Karma & Relationships") in *Astrology, Karma & Transformation;* the first two parts of *Relationships & Life Cycles;* and the author's forthcoming book, *Person-to-Person Astrology: Cosmic Factors in Love, Sex & Compatibility* (due to be published in 1980). This latter book presents a more detailed analysis of the use of the elements in chart comparisons, as well as many other factors involved in doing thorough work in understanding relationships.

16

*The Elements & The Houses:
A Key-Word System*

In this chapter, I am assuming that the reader is already somewhat acquainted with the traditional meanings of the houses found in any elementary astrological textbook. The beginning student of astrology may not immediately grasp the full significance of this key-word system since he would not yet have the experience required to show the need for such an ordering pattern of the houses' principles. However, I urge any beginning student to keep this key-word system in mind as a basis for deeper understanding of the traditional concepts encountered during the course of his studies and while making his first attempts at chart interpretation.

Since this is a book centering primarily on the four elements as the living energies represented in any birth-chart, I should explain here that the correlations between the elements and specific types of houses in this chapter are purely symbolic. Since the houses, by definition, represent the fields of experience wherein the actual energies (or elemental attunements) of the signs and planets operate, the houses should not be seen in any way as a manifestation of the four elements. The primary energies of the chart are indicated always by the placement of the signs and planets. However, since there is a regular and valid correlation between the twelve signs and the twelve houses as two different but parallel sequences of developmental principles, I have herein — in traditional fashion — correlated Aries with the first house, Taurus with the second house, and so on. Nevertheless, the signs and houses should always be seen as distinct and separate factors in the astrological alphabet when one is engaged in interpreting charts.

In the course of teaching dozens of classes in all levels of astrology during the past few years, I have observed that more students have difficulty understanding the nature of the houses than any other aspect of astrological symbolism. Most of the students quickly gained a competent understanding of the signs and planets; but, as soon as the topic of the houses were brought up, I was confronted by numerous confused questions and puzzled expressions. Even those students who seemed to breeze through a class in the fundamentals often wrote back six months later to ask me if I could recommend a good book on the houses since they were meeting many obstacles in their attempt to comprehend this important segment of the astrological language.

It seems to me that the main problem in coming to grips with the meaning of the houses lies in the fact that most astrological texts make no attempt to explain the fundamental principle of each house and the essential inner meaning from which are derived all of the endless associations and ramifications allotted to that house. Most books emphasize the traditional meanings of the houses to the exclusion of the more subtle and more comprehensive principles involved. They do this because most astrologers are still concerned with the environment and the outer situation rather than with the inner experience of the individual. (Dane Rudhyar's recent book *The Astrological Houses* is a rare and welcome exception.) What is not stated by most authors is that the houses — and, indeed, the chart as a whole — always show the inner state and the personal experience much more clearly than the environmental circumstances. This is the reason that so many astrological predictions fail to come about, simply because they are based on the assumption that the chart shows "what is going to *happen*.". The truth is that the chart inevitably shows "what one is going to *experience*." There is an important distinction between these two approaches to astrology, a distinction amply clarified in the works of Rudhyar and other person-centered astrologers.

To interpret a symbolic cosmic language like astrology through the use of our awkward and limited verbal language is a difficult task. This task is made utterly impossible if we assign rigid meanings to the houses; and, in doing so, we are setting up a situation in which we will often have to "stretch" our interpretations to fit the person's specific situation. Such a method of astrological practice merely adds to the justification for many people's supercilious attitude toward all astrological practitioners. As an example of what I mean, suppose a person has Saturn in his natal fifth house. This placement of Saturn can and does indicate a whole variety of attitudes and experience. Hence, what do we say to a person who has this factor in the birth-chart? Would it help the person to say that he will have "trouble with children?" Who, I might add, doesn't have some trouble with children? Such an interpretation is utterly meaningless. Would it be useful to say that the person won't be able to be as creative as he wants to be? This interpretation is also meaningless and, in fact, untrue; for some of the greatest artists and writers of our times have this placement of Saturn. Many other examples could be given to show how totally misleading astrological work can become if we fail to penetrate into the *essential* significance of particular chart factors. On the other hand, if we can sum up the core principle of, in this case, the fifth house as the field of experience wherein one "seeks security for one's own identity," we can then begin to get to the heart of what the person is experiencing, whether it manifests as dealings with a child, lover, creative work, gambling, or whatever. Once the key principle is identified, it is then a relatively easy matter to delineate and understand the specific ways it is being expressed.

It is this need to elucidate the essential psychological significance of the houses that has prompted me to construct the key-word system outlined in this chapter. Many of the words have been used before, by other writers, but in a different context. I have been working with this system for the past three years and am, at this point, satisfied that it does serve as an extremely useful method of not only interpreting the natal chart and the cycles of transits but also coming to a deeper understanding of the entire structure of astrology. Although some of the key-words may at first seem awkward or puzzling, I feel certain that those who take the time to delve into the system and use it consistently will be rewarded for their patience.

House Classification

The most familiar way of defining the different types of houses is to separate them into the classifications of angular, succedent, and cadent. The angular houses are associated with a self-activating quality and have an immediate impact on the structure of one's life. The key-word for the angular houses is *ACTION*. The succedent houses are associated with individual desires and the things we want to control and manage. This urge toward control is motivated by our need for *SECURITY,* the key-word for this type of house. The cadent houses are the sections of the chart where there is input, exchange, and distribution of thoughts and observations. And hence, the key-word for these houses is *LEARNING.* The progression of houses from angular through succedent and cadent and back to angular again symbolizes the flow of life experience: we act, we consolidate the results of our actions in order to attain security; we learn from what we have done and also become aware of what remains to be done; and, therefore we act again. Everyone participates in this cycle of life, but our individual birth-charts reveal which phases in the cycle are dominant in this lifetime.

The houses are also divided according to groups of three, depending upon the element of the signs associated with those houses. For example, the three houses associated with the water signs (4, 8, 12) make up what has been called the "psychic trinity" or the "trinity of soul." For the sake of brevity and simplicity, I'll call these houses simply "the water houses." All of these houses deal with the past, with the conditioned responses which are now instinctual and operate through the emotions. Planets in these houses show what is happening on subconscious levels and indicate the process of gaining consciousness through the *assimilation* of the essence of the past, while simultaneously letting go of the useless memories and fears that hold us back. These "water" houses relate to attaining emotional peace by freeing ourselves from the grip of the past. At the deepest level, these houses symbolize the most profound *yearnings* of the soul; for they indicate the process by which the emotional residue from the past is purged before the soul can express itself clearly and actively.

The keywords for the water houses are, therefore, *EMOTIONAL* and *SOUL*.

The earth houses (2, 6, 10 — often called the "trinity of wealth") are associated with the level of experience wherein we try to satisfy our basic *needs* in the practical world: possessions, money, job, health, reputation, etc. The key-word for these houses is therefore *MATERIAL,* for the earth houses deal chiefly with concerns of the material world.

The fire houses (1, 5, 9 — often called the "trinity of life") are associated with one's attitudes towards life itself, toward the experience of being alive. They represent an outpouring of energy into the world and the aspirations and inspriations that motivate us to do so. The key-word that sums up the essential meaning of the fire houses is *IDENTITY;* for our sense of identity, our sense of *being,* determines out attitude toward life in general. In other words, if we feel good about ourselves, we feel good about being alive; and we therefore develop faith that this life will be an essentially positive experience.

The air houses (3, 7, 11 — called the "trinity of relationship") are associated not only with social contacts and relationships of all types, but also with *concepts.* The social and intellectual realms of activity are inseparable, for it is our concepts that motivate us to seek out other people of like mind, and those very concepts constitute a great part of what is shared between any two people. The key-words for the air houses are, therefore, *SOCIAL* and *INTELLECTUAL*.

The following presents a concise formulation of these key-words:

Mode of Expression		*Level of Experience*	
Angular:	*Action*	Water:	*Soul & Emotional*
Succedent:	*Security*	Earth:	*Material*
Cadent:	*Learning*	Fire:	*Identity*
		Air:	*Social & Intellectual*

The Water Houses

As seen above, all of the water houses have certain things in common, in that they all represent experience on the emotional and soul level. However, analyzing the three modes of expression indicated by the key-words gives us a clue to the interrelationship of these houses.

The Fourth House

The fourth house is the area of direct *ACTION* on the *EMO-TIONAL* and *SOUL* level. All action at this level of experience is necessarily conditioned by factors beyond our control. Traditionally, the fourth house is related to, among other things, the home and family. In what area of life do we act so much on the basis of habit and emotion as when dealing with our family members?

The fourth house also represents our need for privacy, for an environment in which we feel comfortable, in order that we can turn within and relax, recuperate, and reflect without feeling any pressure from the outside world. People who have the Sun in the fourth house generally spend many years trying (whether consciously or unconsciously) to gain freedom from the conditioning associated with their early life experience. In other terms, we could say that those who have a strong emphasis on the fourth house have a need to *act* at the deepest emotional level in order to assimilate the essence of their experience in childhood and youth. They yearn for *peace for the individual self,* which often requires a physical distance from the parents so that they can gain detachment on the emotions aroused by their presence.

The Eighth House

The succedent water house, the eighth, represents the need to find *EMOTIONAL SECURITY* and *SOUL SECURITY*. Those with an emphasis on this house in their birth-charts inevitably involve themselves in activities which, they feel, will provide them with this sort of deep inner stability. The sexuality associated with the eighth house is prompted not merely by instinct, but also by a need to experience ultimate emotional security through merging with another person. Many people attempt to gain this feeling of security by achieving power and influence over others. This power is sometimes provided by wealth or by participation in large corporate ventures, and it sometimes stems from their knowledge of occult laws or from a penetrating psychic sensitivity. Other eighth house matters, such as insurance and joint finances, can also be clearly related to emotional security. The fact that the eighth house is also called the "house of death" points out why people with an eighth house emphasis are often preoccupied with thoughts of death, afterlife, spiritualistic phenomena, and legacies. These people are concerned with such matters because, although they may not recognize it as such, they sense within themselves a longing for soul security, for an assurance that their soul will be "saved."

Although people with eighth house emphasis may seek security in material values, power, sex, or psychic knowledge, a real feeling of emotional and soul security can only exist when the tumultuous emotional conflicts always shown by this house begin to subside. And such emotional turbulence gives way to a deep sense of inner peace only when the true nature of the individual's yearnings are recognized. The occult studies associated with this house are primarily useful as a means of attaining this inner peace through the knowledge of the deepest laws of life. The sexuality of the eighth house is an expression of the urge to be reborn through union with a greater power than self. In short, this house symbolizes a longing for a *state of emotional peace* which can be arrived at only by growing free from desires and compulsive willfulness.

The Twelfth House

The cadent water house, the twelfth, is the area of *LEARNING* on the *EMOTIONAL* and *SOUL* level. This learning takes place through the gradual growth of awareness that accompanies loneliness and deep suffering, through selfless service, or through devotion to a higher ideal. The twelfth house represents influences and experiences which are totally and obviously beyond our control, but which can be transcended by directing our energies toward self-knowledge and spiritual values. It reveals the phase of evolution wherein one must assimilate the results of all past life experiences and responsibilities. And, at the deepest level, this house indicates the urge to seek *peace for the soul* through sur-

render to a higher unity, through devotion to a transcendent
ideal, and through freedom from the ghosts of past thoughts and
actions.

The Earth Houses

The Tenth House

The angular earth house deals with *ACTION* on the *MATE-
RIAL* level; and, traditionally, this house is said to represent
one's reputation, position in the world, and vocation. The action
that anyone performs in the material world is the basis upon
which his reputation rests, and the public categorizes the individual according to what action he is performing: baker, sales-
man, doctor, etc. The key-words also clarify the tenth house's
association with the specific ambition that one hopes to accomplish in the world.

The Second House

The succedent earth house, the second, has for its key-word
MATERIAL SECURITY. This explains why the second house
has been related to money, earnings, possessions, and the desire
to control things and people. However, the key-word also clarifies
the broader principle underlying such inclinations, for many
people with a strong second house emphasis are not so much
concerned with money itself as with an assurance that they will
always be secure in the material world by having an abundance of
resources to draw upon. Thus, many such people collect coins, buy
land, invest in banks and real estate in the attempt to consolidate
their security. I have also noticed that people with the Sun in the
second house are generally rather stingy with their time (especially if the Sun is in a fixed sign), for they feel that their every
effort must be specifically productive of income in some form or
another.

The Sixth House

The cadent earth house is the sixth, and it has been associated
with work, health and duties. When we see that the underlying
principle of the sixth house is that of *LEARNING* through im-

mediate experience with *MATERIAL* affairs, we can easily understand the motivation behind these activities. We learn about our material body's needs and limitations chiefly through health problems (often coming from bad habits, too much pressure from work or duties, or excessive self-criticism or negative thinking — all sixth house matters). We also gain practical insight into ourselves through the everyday performance of our work and duties. All these areas of experience help us to learn humility, to accept our limitations, and to take responsibility for our own state of health, both physical and psychological. When it is understood that the sixth house represents a phase of purification through immediate contact with the material level of experience, we can begin to interpret this house in a true and positive way.

The Fire Houses

The First House

The angular fire house is the first house and represents one's *IDENTITY* in *ACTION*, the phase of life wherein one is identified with specific, self-directed action. People with a strong emphasis on their first house are impatient for action since their sense of self begins to fade if they abstain from active individual involvement with the outer world. Traditionally, this house is also associated with the energy and appearance of the physical body; and, using the key-words, one can see that the body *is* one's identity in action. People recognize us and are influenced by our most characteristic manner of physical movement and expression; and anyone begins to feel devitalized if the qualities shown by the first house planets and the ascendant are suppressed or thwarted.

The Fifth House

The succedent fire house, the fifth, represents the search for *IDENTITY SECURITY*. Those with an emphasis on this house are seeking a secure sense of self by identifying with things or people in which they see themselves reflected. These people *want to be significant* in some way, not simply *to be* as in the first house phase. An emphasis on this house can indicate a self-centered attitude toward life, but it more deeply reveals the individual's emotional attitude and religious *feelings* about all of life. The urge toward significance and the attempt to gain a secure sense of identity are reflected in each matter commonly associated with this house. Children, for example, are often a focus for one's own desires for a secure identity. Not only are many children named after their parents (especially sons being named after the father), but also we have all seen how many parents foist their own desires for recognition and accomplishment upon their children. A person with a strong creative bent (fifth house) finds that he *has* to produce something in order to feel good about himself.

One of the greatest attractions of love affairs (another fifth house matter) is that such a relationship, although it may be totally impractical and often extremely disruptive, gives us a brief experience of self-worth simply because another person has found us worthy to love. In an intense love affair, our sense of identity is confirmed; we see ourselves in the other person; and, because we feel better about ourselves, our outlook on life itself brightens considerably. To sum up, a strong emphasis on the fifth house in the natal chart indicates that the individual must project himself into the world, that he must exercise his creative powers responsibly and consistently in order to attain the sense of joy and security he needs.

The Ninth House

The cadent fire house, the ninth, represents *LEARNING* on the level of *IDENTITY,* in other words, learning who one really is. From this essential principle flow all the religious and philosophical attitudes, searchings, and activities with which this house is usually associated. The motivation behind all religious and philosophical speculation is the need to know own's true identity. The question "Who am I?" is the spring from which every religious quest flows. Therefore, people with an emphasis on this house are drawn to activities which widen their horizons of self-awareness, enable them to improve themselves, and help them to gain a perspective on human nature. Foreign travel and higher mental studies are the beginning stages in this quest. In the next stage, the person identifies himself with a religion, philosophy, or metaphysical doctrine; and thereafter, he often devotes himself to learning directly from a teacher or from an organization which he believes embodies the truth.

The Air Houses

The entire range of personal relationship is represented by these houses, comprising not only the way one approaches various kinds of relationships but also the social urges and intellectual needs that motivate specific types of behavior in these areas.

The Seventh House

The angular air house, the seventh, symbolizes *ACTION* at the *SOCIAL* and *INTELLECTUAL* level. Since one-to-one relationship is the basic meaning of the seventh house, and since all social structures and activities depend upon the quality of such relationship, it is appropriate that the angular air house focuses on this field of experience. More specifically, all advanced societies are founded upon the "marriage" unit, and the stability and efficiency of that social unit to a great extent determines the viability of the social order. On the individual level, the quality of a person's chief partnership has such impact that its influence pervades all the other areas of life: health, finance, children, sex, professional success, etc. (Sociological research exists which indicates that an individual's career often suffers when his marriage breaks up.)

The intellectual aspect of this house can be seen in the way that people with a strongly accented seventh house so readily appeal to the public in their presentation of ideas. Such people are often sought out as consultants, advisors, and counselors purely on the basis of their intellectual competence and objectivity.

The Eleventh House

The succedent air house is the eleventh and represents the search for *SOCIAL* and *INTELLECTUAL SECURITY*. Those whose natal charts focus on the eleventh house invariably tend to associate themselves with others who share their ideas and objectives. This is so because they feel socially and intellectually insecure and therefore find great comfort in the knowledge that there are other people who can understand and accept them as they are. These people often join groups or align themselves with friends who share their intellectual bent, although they may not agree at all on specifics. Their search for intellectual security also leads them into vast systems of thought, whether political, metaphysical, or scientific. These people have a marked ability to facilitate group activities, social change ventures, and the "management" of large masses of people.

The mental rigidity so common in these people stems from the fact that they are intellectually insecure and therefore extremely hesitant to change their ideas once they find concepts that satisfy them. (It is an interesting sidelight that an Aquarian president, F.D.R., devised the system known as "Social Security"; and the eleventh house is naturally correlated with Aquarius.) The most effective way that a person with a strong eleventh house can achieve the security he seeks is to establish a strong sense of individual *purpose* which not only fulfills his personal needs but also *harmonizes with the needs of society as a whole*. To avoid the rigidity and opinionated characteristics of this house, he would do well to focus on the purpose itself rather than upon oversimplified concepts that purport to state absolute truth. In that way, he can apply his ideas concretely toward the amelioration of society.

The Third House

The cadent air house, the third, is the field of *LEARNING* on the *INTELLECTUAL* and *SOCIAL* level. It therefore represents all forms of exchange of information, such as basic communication skills, media work, merchandizing, sales, etc. Those with a third house emphasis have an insatiable need to communicate with others and an ability to deal in an easy and friendly way with people of the most diverse qualities and interests. Their curiosity about people and ideas is endless; and this inquisitiveness leads them to make numerous casual acquaintances and to evolve a broad and flexible intellectual background. Basic facts and abstract ideas are both important to these people, even if such

information is isolated from any "significant" context. Whereas
the learning represented by the ninth house comes about through
the use of the inspired intuitive mind, the learning of the third
house occurs through the application of one's own logic and reason.

Astrology: A Tool for Self-Knowledge

After having used this key-word system for a while, it will
become apparent that it is valuable not only for understanding
the general life pattern shown in the natal chart, but also that it
makes the meaning of current and future trends and cycles much
more accurate and psychologically significant. For example, if a
particular birth-chart has a lack of the air element as indicated
by planetary placement, why is it that this person is so interested
in people and continually involves himself in social activities? An
emphasis on the air houses will reveal that, although he may not
have an *energy attunement* to that element, he still may focus
some of his water, fire, or earth energy toward social, intellectual,
and relationship *activities*. Or if a person has no attunement to
the fire element, why is it that she seems to exemplify the high-
spirited and optimistic qualities that she supposedly lacks? An
emphasis on the fire houses in her chart indicates that, although
she does not have the energy attunement to the fire element, she
nevertheless pours her air, water and earth energies into inspired, creative, and idealistic fields of experience.

In cases like those mentioned above, the individual will still
lack attunement to a certain element and will usually still manifest some of the problems associated with that lack. However,
since the sorts of activities that interest them compensate to some
extent for their elemental imbalance, such people will often experience a more moderate form of the expected difficulty. It is
only by a patient and detailed examination of the entire birth-
chart that the astrologer can evaluate the degree in which one
astrological factor compensates or balances off another. If, however, a particular person lacks emphasis on the water signs *and*

the water houses, for example, one can almost be assured that the problem indicated has reached a severe degree of imbalance.

In the area of understanding transits, progressions, Key Cycles, and similar projection techniques, the astrologer who uses this system will no longer have to choose one of the many possible meanings of, for example, transiting Jupiter or Saturn in a certain house, leaving the distinct possibility that the main point will be entirely missed. He will be able to know with confidence that the advice and explanations he gives will help clients to look within themselves for the real meaning of a particular time period, rather than encouraging them to focus on some trivial or non-existent event. By clarifying the basic principle involved in a particular phase of life experience, a principle that invariably pertains to the situation regardless of the surface conditions that the client may talk about, the astrological practitioner will be able to eliminate much of the usual guesswork and to avoid being misled by the client's lack of perspective or self-deception. In short, the utilization of this key-word system can be in actual practice one more step in making astrology what it should be: a tool for promoting self-knowledge.

Appendices, References, & Suggested Readings

APPENDIX A

Scientific Data

The following lists numerous reports of research and experiments which deal directly or indirectly with astrological premises. Although none of the experiments can be considered conclusive proof of astrology's validity, the results listed below do indicate a growing support in scientific circles for traditional astrological correspondences between the terrestrial and celestial spheres.

1. According to modern thought in physics, matter exists in four states: solid, liquid, gas, and plasma, which correspond precisely with the astrological elements: earth, water, air, and fire.

2. Dr. Eugen Jonas, a Czechoslovakian psychiatrist and gynecologist, has since 1956 been working toward the establishment of definite relationships between the period of a woman's optimal time for conception and the phase of the moon that occured at her birth. He has also found that a child conceived when there is an opposition of the sun and any larger planet (i.e., when the sun and the planet were 180⁰ in longitude from each other) has a much greater chance of suffering birth defects, miscarriage, mental retardation, and other factors which negatively affect his health. There is a thorough report of Dr. Jonas' work in the book *Astrological Birth Control* by Sheila Ostrander and Lynn Schroeder (Englewood Cliffs, N.J.: Prentice-Hall, 1972).

3. Scientists at Sandia Laboratories in Albuquerque, New Mexico have released a publication called "Intriguing Accident Patterns Plotted Against a Background of Natural Environment Features," in which they state that accident rates — and presumably other manifestations of human behavior — are influenced by phases of the moon, solar cycles, and other natural phenomena. Further research revealed that the variations in the magnetic field around the Albuquerque area seemed to correspond closely to increases and decreases in the accident rate. (Reported in *Time*, January 10, 1972)

4. The semi-monthly Newsletter of the Knoll Pharmaceutical Company, *Hospital Focus*, reports:

   ... the heavenly bodies have distinguishable effects on biologic materials. At the present state of knowledge, this thesis has become testable, and has apparently been verified, at least in broad outline.

   The case for celestial influence rests on several pillars: Electromagnetic phenomena can be shown to be associated in some ways with biologic processes; the terrestrial electro-magnetic environment is subject to variations induced by other electromagnetic events in the solar system.

   ... What it is that causes geomagnetic variations has never been completely clear but, in addition to solar activity, recent research relates it to lunar phases.

Doubts and statistical puzzles to one side, however, it is an almost inescapable conclusion that it will eventually be shown exactly in what ways magnetic fields in biologic matter may interact with magnetic fields in their environment.

What it is that causes solar changes is still not known, but one possibility involves disturbances caused by the planets. The angle Jupiter-Sun-Saturn is approximately 0 or 180° every 11 years, roughly in time with a major solar cycle. (Reported in *Hospital Focus,* February 15, 1965)

5. Professor Frank A. Brown, Morrison Professor of Biology at Northwestern University, has shown conclusively that plants and animals are capable of responding to changes in the earth's magnetic atmosphere, which changes are caused by the sun, moon, and possibly the planets. Although science can't find the "mechanism" used to accept and interpret geomagnetic signals, Brown points out that science has never identified the mechanism involved in the sense of smell either. Brown states that the response to inner "cosmic clocks" or biological clocks is derived "through a continuous response of the living organism to its rhythmic geophysical environment." ("Living Clocks", *Science,* CXXX (1959, 1535). In fact, Brown states that "living things cannot live without timegivers from space." (*ibid.*) Brown also found that oysters and rats were responsive to the celestial environment, even when isolated from any direct contact with it. For example, he found that rats kept in a cloud room were always most active when the moon was beneath the horizon and least active when the moon was above the horizon. Since Brown's work, we can see that it is impossible to have "controlled" laboratory conditions. (Reported in *Today's Health,* October, 1971; "How the Heavens Influence Our Lives" by Martin Cohen.)

6. Russian Scientists have correlated the extent of flu epidemics throughout the world with the 11 year sunspot cycle mentioned in #4 above. (Reported in *London Sunday Times,* July 18th, 1971).

7. In the January, 1971 issue of *Kosmobiologie,* H.E. Parker reports that research workers at the Institute for Cosmic Ray Research in Indiana have discovered that not only sunspots but also certain cosmic energy conditions and their cosmic rays may influence life and health, death and disease. Moreover, each month has its own rhythms which, it is suggested, should be indicated on every calendar so that everyone may take advantage of them. Professor Dylhusen, a Danish research scientist in the US, and a specialist in cosmic ray research, has confirmed that hitherto unknown factors play a part in the body's capacity for re-charging itself! For example, in cases where one's health is gone due to overstrain, certain cosmic rays apparently come into play to ensure sufficient rest and sleep.

8. Doctors Bureau and Craine claim to have established a definite correlation between harmonies of the sunspot cycle and complex combinations of the periods of Jupiter, Saturn, Uranus, and Neptune, the four largest planets. It is pointed out that many different

terrestrial events have been correlated with the sunspot cycles, e.g., wheat crop successes, flu epidemics, business cycles, etc. (Reported in *Nature,* May 12, 1970, page 984).

9. Edgar R. Wagner, Ph.D., a research chemist who has studied astrology for over fifty years, writes:

> The earth thus appears in space not only as an isolated planet with a solid core, but also as a complex living composit of all the actions of, and the reactions to, these influences, surrounded by an aura of invisible but exactly delimited shells of electrical, magnetic, and corpuscular nature. It is therefore not only not surprising, but cannot be expected to be otherwise, that this sensitive cosmic structure that is pulsating with every form of energy, reacts directly or indirectly to planetary forces. (*Kosmos,* Vol. 1, #9 (August, 1970, p. 15)

10. Professor Rudolph Tomaschek, the internationally known geophysicist from the University of Munich, writes:

> I emphasize the adjective "modern" in connection with "scientist" in order to avoid the idea of this being merely one who is prepared to observe the processes of nature in an unbiased manner, but rather one who has also overcome the materialistic viewpoint and has recognized that the structure of Nature, in that part of it that can be investigated by natural science, is a structure composed of fields of force whose energy, in the final analysis, is probably a dynamic network of frequencies whose carrier remains unknown and undefinable. . . . It follows that the earth's surface is continually involved in a constantly changing flow of gratitational, electric and magnetic fields, both external, from the sun, moon, and planets, and from the earth's own electro-magnetic field. (from monograph "Cosmic Force Fields and Astral Influence")

11. Clinical psychologist Vernon Clark designed some interesting and challenging tests for astrology and astrologers in 1959 and the early 1960's. A group of 20 astrologers and a control group of 20 psychologists and social workers were the participants in the series of tests. The first test required the participants to discriminate between a true horoscope and a spurious one. The astrologers came up with results that would occur by chance less than once in one thousand times. Three astrologers had perfect scores, eighteen scored above chance, two scored at chance, and none scored below chance. The control group scored almost exactly at chance. (Reported in *Aquarian Agent,* Vol. 1, No. 9 (August, 1970), p. 22)

12. The prediction of solar flares has become vitally important to the space program. Hence, Dr. Richard Head of the Electronics Research Center of NASA was reported in the May 15, 1967 issue of "Technology Weekly" as having developed an electronic computer technique for predicting solar flares using the gravitational vectors of Mercury, Venus, Jupiter, and Saturn. These solar flares affect our weather and perhaps other things also.

13. John H. Nelson, a radio-weather forecaster employed by RCA Communications, Inc., announced in March of 1951 that, after five years of research, he had developed a technique using the angular config-

urations of the planets to predict disturbances in radio communications. Although Nelson admits that he doesn't know what forces from the planets affect the earth's atmosphere, his forecasts, done months in advance, are accurate over 85% of the time. His practical use of planetary angles provides the most convincing proof available of the important astrological concept of the "aspects" between planets. (See Nelson's book *Cosmic Patterns* for details. It is published by the American Federation of Astrologers, 1974.)

14. The American Institute of Medical Climatology in Philadelphia, working with police and fire departments, major hospitals, several large industrial corporations, and the University of Pennsylvania Medical School, conducted a three-year study (1959-61) of human reactions to the phases of the moon. Their conclusions were that cases of murder, rape, aggravated assault, and arson are most common during full moon periods. Their findings related that celestial events like full moon, eclipses, or simply conjunctions of planets are directly related to the ion count in the atmosphere, barometric pressure, amount of moisture in the air, and other terrestrial factors, some of which are not clearly understood. (Similar findings are mentioned in A.D. Pokorny's "Moon Phases, Suicide, and Homicide" in the *American Journal of Psychiatry*, 121; July, 1964, pp. 66-67; and in S.F. Bauer's "Lunar Effects on Mental Illness: The Relationship of Moon Phase to Psychiatric Emergencies" in *American Journal of Psychiatry*, 125; November, 1968, pp. 696-97.)

15. Surgeons Drs. Carl S. McLemore and Edson Andrews pooled the graphs of excessive bleeders over a period of eight years. They reported in *The Journal of the Florida Medical Association* that hemorrhaging dropped to a monthly low at new moon and reached a peak each month as the moon opposed the sun (full moon).

16. A great deal of important research has been done by Dr. Robert O. Becker, an orthopedic surgeon at the State University of New York's Upstate Medical Center in Syracuse. First of all, he has found that the frequency of psychiatric hospital admissions correlates highly with the geomagnetic field intensity. His research was reported in the British scientific weekly *Nature* after studying over 28,000 admissions. The correlation in this case was so strong that the probability of its occurrence by chance alone was less than 1 in 10,000. In other research, he has shown that, in several respects, biologic tissue (and especially the nervous system) acts like a solid state system of semiconductors. Becker writes:

> Every organism, including the human organism, demonstrates cycles of biological and mental-emotional activity closely linked to geo-magnetic force-field patterns and more complex force-field interrelations, both planetary and solar-terrestrial in scope. Human behavior is influenced through the direct current central system of the brain by the terrestrial magnetic field, solar and planetary conditions, and both high and low energy cosmic radiation.

At present, we can only suspect a general relationship of some kind between the whole of the human species and the whole of the electromagnetic phenomenon that engages the sun, other stars, and galaxies.

Reports of Dr. Becker's work are found in the following:

1) Becker, Bachman, & Friedman: "Relation Between Natural Magnetic Field Intensity and the Incidence of Psychiatric Disturbances in the Human Population", presented at the International Conference on High Magnetic Fields; Cambridge, Mass., June 16, 1961.

2) Becker, R.O. "Relationship of Geomagnetic Environment to Human Biology", *New York State Journal of Medicine,* 63, 2215 (August 1, 1963).

3) Becker, R.O. "The Physiologic Mechanism of Action of Magnetic Fields on Neural Structures," presented at the New York Academy of Sciences, November 12, 1962.

17. In a statistical study of astrological indications of compatibility between married couples, psychologist-astrologer Leslie Furze-Morrish (*In Search*, fall, 1959) demonstrated a clear relationship between compatible couples and a predominance of 120° and 60° aspects between planets in their two charts. The 120° and 60° angular relationship between two planets has been known among astrologers to indicate mutual harmony of energies and qualities since before Ptolemy. In addition, the planets Venus and Jupiter (the traditional "benefic" planets of ancient astrology) were found to be more prominent in the chart comparisons than other planets. Likewise, Furze-Morrish reported a corresponding relationship between incompatible couples and a predominance of mutual 180° and 90° aspects between planets in the two charts, which angular relationships are the two traditionally most stressful or discordant. Additionally, the planet Mars was found to be the most prominent in these charts, giving support to the astrological assumption that Mars (the ancient god of war) generates or correlates with strife, conflict, and quarrels. This research, plus that of Nelson at RCA, plus that of Jonas in Czechslovakia (showing non-viable conceptions occurring at 180° angles of planets) all reveal convincing support for the astrological theory of "aspects" between planets, which theory is the foundation for the interpretation of planets' "strength" or "weakness" in an individual chart.

18. The reader should also refer to West and Tooner's *The Case for Astrology* (which lists other relevant data) and Michel Gauquelin's books: *Cosmic Clocks, The Scientific Basis of Astrology*, and *Cosmic Influences on Human Behavior.*

APPENDIX B
Astrology & Modern Research In Energy Fields

Research in many fields (especially physics, psychology, and medicine) is increasingly concerned with the "energy" aspect of life and of the individual human being. Although we can choose to see astrology as "merely" a symbolic language, we must admit that symbols are *symbols* precisely because they refer to some reality which is otherwise inexpressible or incomprehensible to human consciousness. The rather transcendent reality referred to by astrological symbols is "energy," a term which is hard to define although everyone speaks of it and experiences it. Not only physicists, but also the more progressive members of the healing professions, are increasingly referring to energy as the fundamental reality underlying all particular manifestations. The reason why astrology is the most complete and accurate symbolic language, as well as the most useful diagnostic tool in the healing and counseling arts, is because astrology is essentially a *language of energy*, thus enabling practitioners in these fields to differentiate accurately between all the various energies operating in the human psycho-physical organism. Astrology, as the most complete language of energy known to man, can be for the healing arts what the periodic table is for chemistry. And, in the field of parapsychological research, it can help to unify our understanding of such diverse phenomena as auras, ESP, and altered states of consciousness.

The following list includes various aspects of current research into the "energy" dimension of life, and I feel that any attempt to unify the findings in such diverse fields would necessitate the use of a comprehensive and precise language of energy, such as astrology.

1. Quoted from the April, 1971 issue of the ARE News:

   The new focus of medical science is on electrophysiology. Case Western Reserve University is now using electrical impulses to treat backache, sclerosis, and to minimize the pain from terminal cancer.

   Electricity is generated in the body by the movement of muscles. There is so much electricity in human blood that we can harness it and use it to run a motor! Scientists have learned that they can submerge two tiny electrodes in a beaker of human blood and electricity flows therefrom.

2. Dr. Lloyd Graham of Grants Pass, Oregon, who uses magnetism in the treatment of illness and injury, writes:

   The human body is a wonderful and orderly arrangement of electromagnetic light wave vibrational patterns in gravitational and radiational motion. (Goodavage, J. *Astrology: The space age science.* New York: Signet, 1967, p. 137.)

3. Wolf (In Disease as a way of life: Neural integration in systemic pathology. *Perspectives in biological medicine*, 1961, 4, 288-305) states that both health and illness are aspects of man's way of life. Thus, disease is not a special state or a temporary derangement but rather a

part of man's state of being. This approach regards symptoms as temporary flareups or intensifications of continuing energy processes within the individual, in the same way as astrological transits produce (or correspond with) intensifications of experiences, energy flow, or discord indicated as potential in the natal horoscope. Numerous studies have, in fact, shown that physical "dis-ease" manifest particularly during times of mental or emotional stress.

4. Recent research in the Soviet Union points toward the existence of an "unknown energy factor" other than electro-magnetic energy. Various experiments in the Soviet Union dealing with ESP and clairvoyance (labeled "biological radio communication") point toward "the hypothesis ... that telepathic transmission is accomplished by some kind of energy or factor so far unknown to us yet belonging to the highest stage in the development of matter ....." (Reported in R. Schaffranke. Telepathy: A science of the future. ARE Journal, 1970, 5 (6), pp. 215-220.) Soviet research finds that this energy is (1) independent of distance, (2) achieved without the use of the senses, (3) has no apparent relation to electro-magnetic waves, and (4) contradicts the "law" of causality.

Another report (Jackson, J.H. *Pictorial Guide to the Planets*. New York: Crowell, In press.) points out that the Mariner II flyby of Venus revealed that the planet has little or no magnetic field, suggesting that if the planetary cause of sun-spot activity is substantiated, the effect is probably neither wholly gravitational nor magnetic. Both of these reports point toward an energy factor that might be made to account for astrological "influence" and toward a dimension of activity that transcends the known laws of gravity, magnetism, electricity, and time-space causality.

5. Two books by Sheila Ostrander and Lynn Schroeder (*Psychic Discoveries Behind the Iron Curtain* and *Astrological Birth Control*) include many reports of research into the energy dimension of physical, psychological, and parapsychological phenomena. Although too numerous to mention all of them here, the following give some idea of how wide-spread this new area of research has become. (Both books also contain extensive bibliographies of research on human energy fields.)

a. Dr. Harold Burr, Professor of Neuroanatomy at Northwestern University, "established in 1935 that all living matter, from a tiny seed to a human being, is surrounded and controlled by electrodynamic fields which are in turn affected by the moon and sun ..... Burr's findings seem to imply that the electrodynamic fields of the entire body are involved in ovulation." For millenia, the Chinese acupuncturists have claimed that factors in the environment, including the sun and moon, have profound effects on the fields of energy. (p. 70; *ABC*)

b. At the Institute of Clinical Physiology in Kiev, Russia, it has been demonstrated that the "bioenergies circulating along these acupuncture points on the skin react instantaneously to activities on the sun such as solar flares. The moment a solar flare erupts, the electrical potential of the acupuncture points on the skin rises. The skin reacts virtually simultaneously with the events on the sun *before* the cosmic particles released by the explosion reach the earth one day later." (p. 71; *ABC*)

c. Burr and his colleagues, particularly Dr. Leonard Ravitz, have come up with a new model of living things as "steady-state electrical systems." They speak of "electric tides" in the atmosphere from the sun and moon and their influence on the steady state of organisms. In an article called "Periodic Changes in Electromagnetic Fields" (*Annals of the New York Academy of Science*, LCVIII (1960), 1181.), Ravitz writes that he has found that the action of the sun and moon affect the energy field surrounding each of us. Similar findings are reported by Dr. Becker (See Appendix A), to the effect that subtle changes in the earth's magnetic fields ("caused" by the sun, moon, and planets) actually alter the force field of the human body, which in turn affects the nervous system.

In the April 1959 issue of the *American Journal of Clinical Hypnosis*, Ravitz writes: ". . . the living organism *pulsates* to individually-timed rhythmic variations, whose intensities, elasticities, and directions are amplified, condensed, accelerated, decelerated, and reversed in accord with other frequencies. Beyond all this frenetic energy ebb and flow, the moon remains silently aloof, itself propelled . . . along invisible tracks . . . by the same forces operating upon and within living matter." (p. 72; *ABC*)

d. A section of *Psychic Discoveries* deals with the discovery and photographing of specific "forms of energy" or "energy patterns" which in fact constitute the real life of any organic whole. The fact that this essential energy pattern in every living thing determines the material *form* that we apprehend with the senses points to the fact that some kind of invisible organizing pattern is inherent in living things, just as L.L. Whyte writes in his book *Accent on Form* (see Chapter 4). This is what Dane Rudhyar has for years called the "seed-pattern" shown in the birth-chart. It is simply this organizing pattern within each human being that astrology revelas and symbolically graphs.

e. "The late Dr. Gustaf Stromberg, an American astronomer of world reknown, was one of the first to go into this idea of rhythms and frequencies. He postulated the idea that the structure of living organisms is determined by 'wave systems' or plusing 'electrodynamic living fields'. These fields seem to be the matrix which gives living matter its form and shape by organizing the molecules into complex forms of plants, animals, and humans. Wounds heal, and damaged organs rebuild themselves to their original symmetry. This implies a stabilizing energy pattern responsible for shaping living tissue." (p. 125; *ABC*)

" 'We can compare a living field with a melody,' Stromberg says. A melody is a time sequence of frequencies. The melody is the same whether it is played slow or fast, loud or soft. In the same way, the living fields of a growing embryo retain the same pattern of frequencies as it undergoes great changes in size and eventually grows to become a mature human being. In the human egg cell, Stromberg postulated, the fields could be imagined as existing in extremely contracted and dormant form, almost as a pre-physical potentiality." In Stromberg's view, the physical body of living things is not the *cause* of the fields of energy, but the *result*. (pp. 125-26; *ABC*)

f. Dr. Eugen Jonas of Czechoslovakia states that "an individual, at the moment of creation, accepts a basic impulse from the universe, a sort of vibrational range that will be more or less permanent with respect to its organism. In other words, when the sperm and ovum unite to create new life, the organizing force fields of the fertilized egg are set cycling by the frequencies of the energy wave patterns of the universe at that particular instant. If the patterns are unusually favorable, the individual will be extremely vital . . . . Jonas suggests that the configurations in the cosmos are part of the imprint forming the frequency pattern of a human at the beginning of his life." (p. 127;*ABC*)

g. "Acupuncturists believe Vital Energy in the body links man with the cosmos. If there is a change in the universe and environment, a *resonance* is produced in the Vital Energy of the human body which in turn affects the physical body." (p. 229; *Psychic Discoveries*)

h. The total effect of modern Soviet research in parapsychology is to lead one to assume that the human energy field "reacts to thought, emotion, sound, light, color, magnetic fields, any subtle change in the environment from the grass we walk on to the planets we rarely notice." (p. 234; *PD*)

6. The current interest in energy fields is really not concerned with a new phenomenon. Not only have Indian yogic systems referred for millenia to the *kundalini* (a kind of libido comprising both physical, psychic, and potentially spiritual energy) and to *chakras* (centers of whirling energy within man), but many clairvoyants have reported seeing the "aura" of individuals from which they can deduce the person's state of psychological and physical health. Clairvoyant Eileen Garrett writes:

> I am convinced that every living organism has its own type of external being by which it contacts other energies . ¦ .. This "magnetic" mesh, then, is a map through which illness of the body and mind can be reached and studied by those who understand its principles and functions. (*Adventures in the Supernormal*. New York: Creative Age Press, 1949, p. 173.)

> Since the magnetic field interpenetrates the physical body and also reaches out to relate itself to other energies in the universe, man becomes closely linked to all the cosmic forces that play upon our planet through his magnetic field. (*ibid.*, p. 174.)

This last quotation seems to refer to the same reality that Soviet research has recently encountered. (See section 5-h. in this appendix.)

One might conclude from this last idea that the astrological birth-chart symbolizes the specific attunements of the individual to cosmic forces, thus establishing at birth the basic frequency, rhythm, and resonance of his particular energy field. As Garrett writes, "The 'nativity' of any substance marks its nature and its natural destiny, and, in the case of manufactured things, their making and the purpose for which they were made." (*ibid.*, p. 175.)

7. A great many systems of healing utilize no other tools than the actual energies of the patient and the healer. (The difference between "medicine" and "healing" becomes clear when we realize that the words "heal" and "whole" are etymologically related. Hence, a true system of healing is concerned with restoring the patient to a state of wholeness, whereas much of modern medical practice ignores the question of wholeness and concentrates on superficial symptoms.) The following quotation from Arthur Ford gives a clue of how certain healing systems work:

> That the human body gives radiation has been known scientifically since 1923, when it was measured by the Leningrad scientist Alexander Gurwitsch. George W. Crile demonstrated in 1934 that brain tissue gives off radiation in the visible, infra-red, and ultra-violet ranges. The strongest human radiations — reported the Cornell researcher Dr. O.H. Rahn — emanates from the fingertips of the right hand. . . .. (*Unknown but Known*, 1974, p. 61.)

This fact might explain why "laying on of hands" has been a respected healing method in many cultures and religions, as well as why the right hand is usually considered to be the "positive" hand. Dr. Randolph Stone, whose healing system called "Polarity Therapy" uses nothing more than the two hands and the two people's energies, writes:

> Our research in Psychiatry would benefit greatly if we could reduce this jumble of man's mental-emotional impulses to an *exact science of mental-emotional anatomy, coordinated with the physical one.* Then a sound Psycho-physiology and even a Pathology of these finer energy fields could be established. This would be a great step forward in the science of understanding the mystery of man's complex being, which defies all present man-made rules and findings. (*Polarity Therapy.* Pub. by author, 1954, p. 14.)

APPENDIX C
Astrology & Polarity Therapy

There is an exchange of energy in everything, a rhythmic pulsation of contraction and expansion which enables us to recognize that a plant, animal, or person is "alive." Even the teeth and bones participate in this vital exhange of energy with the universal supply. All substance results from the unlimited combination of energy frequencies, and the basic energies at work have been termed the four humours, the four elements, or have been together designated as Qi, Prana, Mana, Vital Force, and other names depending on the culture concerned. Every living plant, animal, and human being *is* a complex energy field operating simultaneously at many levels, and each must maintain its own individual frequency in order to ensure its growth and development. At birth, the first breath initiates our direct supply of energy, our life-line with the Universal Power, our immediate attunement with the cosmos. So long as our particular energy pattern is well established and flows without obstruction, we are in tune with the Universal supply of life force, and we experience this state of being as one of perfect health and emotional well-being. However, due to physical, mental, or emotional shocks, improper diet, or negative emotional-mental patterns, most of us live in a state of constant tension and wind up feeling "out of tune." In other words, the energy currents that enliven us become blocked, imbalanced, or out of phase, and we therefore feel pain, sickness, fatigue, or depression.

Naturally, there is no life without tension; no one can deal with the material world without experiencing stress. Polarity Therapy is not based on the illusion that one can achieve a state of constant relaxation and an end to all conflicts. It is rather based on the fact that most people are capable of utilizing their energies more effectively, waste a good deal of energy merely in the effort to block the expression of some energies, and can work through their conflicting experiences with more awareness and centeredness than they have done in the past. Polarity Therapy is based on the fact that the mind, emotions, and physical body work together and have a mutual interaction. For example, not only do the emotions and thoughts affect the body, but also the diet, physical environment, and general state of health have a profound impact on the inner state of being. During treatment with a qualified Polarity Therapist, the emotions, thoughts, diet, exercise, living habits, and spiritual inclinations are all taken into consideration; the treatment is holistic, and of course the birthchart is invaluable in understanding the wholeness of the client, his particular needs, yearnings, conflicts, physical weaknesses, and so forth.

The human energy field is now a scientific fact which Acupuncture, Kirlian Photography, and other research have forced orthodox science to recognize. Of course, this living energy field concept of man is nothing new. Psychics have been seeing "auras" for millenia and have been using the aura to diagnose physical, mental, and emotional problems. Unfortunately, we nowadays get so much "education" that we early in life forget what is real. Our minds become cluttered with so much useless information and so many dead mental concepts that it takes years to re-establish our original sensitivity to the energies which manifest through all life. Polarity Therapy is a way of working immediately with life energies, an education in how the life forces operate, as well as a therapeutic tool of amazing power. The essence of Polarity Therapy is elegant in its simplicity, although on the surface it seems to the novice like a mind-boggling science that can never be mastered. In this way, it is like astrology: a system so simple and unified in its essence that it takes many years of practice to perceive its simplicity.

Polarity Therapy is a way of working with the fundamental energies of life, a way of bringing these currents (air, fire, earth, and water) to a state of balance and removing obstructions to their free flow throughout the total energy field. Polarity Therapy is one of very few systems in the healing arts that enables the practitioner to work immediately with the energies symbolized by the individual birth-chart. Enabling this state of flowing balance to establish itself allows the energies themselves to bring about whatever healing needs to be done. The therapist is by no means a healer; he simply stimulates the client's own healing forces to assert themselves. The balanced condition resulting from a Polarity Therapy treatment can expect to experience a marked degree of very deep relaxation, as well as heightened awareness of his or her fundamental needs, energies, and potentials for growth.

The clairvoyant Eileen Garrett in her book *Awareness* has described energy centers in the human body identical to the chakras of yoga traditions and to the concepts expressed in Dr. Stone's books. She states: "Though there are many therapies, there is but one kind of healing. Whether one treats a man in his physical organism or in his psychological states, one aims at the reintegration of the forces of his life." These life forces are considered by Dr. Stone to be the very four elements that comprise the foundation of all astrological theory. The elements are correlated with specific functions physically and psychologically and also with certain energy centers (chakras) in the total energy field. According to Dr. Stone, the four elements (called the "tattwas" in Sanskrit) "are the field and structural tissues of anatomy. They support the life winds of 'prana' that flow through our body." They are the invisible builders of all life's structures and must operate in harmony with one another if the person is to have good health.

Ed. Note: Dr. Stone's works are now being reissued in new editions. His book *Health Building: The Conscious Art of Living Well* is an inexpensive paperback that includes all his writings on diet, vitalizing exercises, and basic health principles. This book is accessible to anyone and includes over 50 illustrations of his exercises and photos of Dr. Stone. For those who want to study the basic energy principles he elaborated and/or Polarity Therapy, the 2-volume set *POLARITY THERAPY: The Complete Collected Works* includes all his written works on the subject and over 100 charts and diagrams illustrating energy patterns and principles as well as specific therapeutic techniques. Write to publisher of this book, CRCS Publications, for complete information.

The Four Elements

In Polarity Therapy (and also in Ayurvedic Medicine), the element *air* is associated with the nervous system, mind sensation, perception, and expression. *Fire* is the warming, energizing principle of the circulatory system. The fire current manifests as the light of the eyes and heat of the brain (Aries), the fire of digestion in the solar plexus area (Leo), and the motor energy in the thighs (Sagittarius). The air current is especially active in the lungs and as intelligence expressed through the hands (Gemini), in the kidney area (Libra), and it electrically charges the body in the ankle area (Aquarius). *Water* is the soothing, cooling, healing and nurturing principle which expresses itself through all the secreting glands and mucous membranes (e.g. Cancer rules the breasts traditionally, Scorpio the genitals and nose, and Pisces the lymph system.) The element *earth* refers to the gross matter of the body, to the physical form of the individual, and to the assimilation and elimination of earthly matter needed to sustain the physical body. Traditionally Capricorn rules the bones, teeth, and skin; Taurus is immediately attuned to the tangible forms of all earthly things; and Virgo is associated with the intestines.

Dr. Stone says that an understanding of these fundamental energies "is the foundation of the mystery of the link between Consciousness and Matter." He points out that general medical practice today is grossly physical rather than atomic in its principles and application. And yet, as astrology makes clear, the actual life cycle of any living creature begins as a process of specific lines of force, specific energy attunements which are liberated according to a specific seed pattern. Dr. Stone's criticism of modern mechanistic medicine could be applied equally to the general practice of Medical Astrology, for most practitioners who deal with this field tend to isolate specific organs, body areas, and names of "diseases" which in reality does very little good. A more constructive approach to medical astrology and to the practice of the healing arts themselves would be to focus on the *function* and the *process* that is disturbed.

As an example, to know that Libra "rules" the kidneys doesn't provide us with much understanding or with any means of preventing kidney trouble. But to realize that the sign Libra and the kidneys are associated with the *air* current energy flow, and to know that this energy can be stimulated, altered, and redirected can open our eyes to an entirely new approach to healing, an approach concerned with the fundamental energies that enliven all creation. Such an approach can provide us with a unified and holistic theory of health, "dis-ease," and healing. Dis-ease is not a special state but rather part of man's way of being; it may be regarded as a temporary flare-up or intensification of ongoing processes. An approach to medical astrology on the level of energy can give us a key to the continuing processes animating each of us; and astrology gives us a language with which we can describe types of energy as well we specific energy dynamics.

References for Part I

Chapter 1

Einstein, A. *Ideas and opinions.* New York: Crown Publishers, 1954.

Freud, S. Quoted in Unitarian-Universalist Psi Symposium Transcripts, 1970.

Kepler, J. *Somnium.* Madison: Univer. of Wisconsin Press, 1967.

Marrone, R.L. *Consciousness and evolution: A radical introduction to psychology.* (Unpublished manuscript, Sacramento State College), 1971.

Oppenheimer, R. Lecture at American Psychological Association Convention, 1971.

Rudin, J. *Psychotherapy and religion.* South Bend, Ind.: Notre Dame University Press, 1968.

Smith, H. Editorial in *The Cooperator,* 1971, 1, pp. 1-4.

Stossel, H. *Cosmobiology,* 1959, July 25.

Whyte, L.L. *Accent on form.* New York: Harper & Bros., 1954.

Chapter 2

Goethe, J. *Faust.* Trans. by Bayard Taylor. New York: Modern Library, 1950.

Goodavage, J. *Astrology: The space age science.* New York: Signet, 1967.

Jeans, J. *The mysterious universe.* New York: Macmillan, 1932.

Laucks, I. Editorial in *The Cooperator,* 1971, 1, p. 5.

Mowrer, O.H. "Sin," the lesser of two evils, In M. Zax & G. Stricker (Eds.), *The study of abnormal behavior.* (2nd ed.) New York: Macmillan, 1969.

Rudin, J. *Psychotherapy & religion.* South Bend, Ind.: Notre Dame Univer. Press, 1968.

Chapter 3

Crebo, Anna. Creativity, psychology, and the cosmos. *The Journal of Astrological Studies,* 1970, 1, 74-83.

Dobyns, Zipporah. The integration of humanistic psychology and astrology. *Kosmos,* 1971, 4 (1), 8-10.

Goethe, J. Quoted in L.L. Whyte. *Accent on form.* New York: Harper & Bros., 1954.

Jung, C.G. *The undiscovered self.* New York: Mentor, 1958.

May, R., Angel, E., & Ellenberger, H.F. (Eds.) *Existence: A new dimension in psychiatry and psychology.* New York: Basic Books, 1958.

May, R. Existential bases of psychotherapy. In M. Zax & G. Stricker (Eds.), *The study of abnormal behavior.* (2nd ed.) New York: Macmillan, 1969.

Rudhyar, D. The part of fortune. Lecture given at American Federation of Astrologers Convention, Boston, 1964.

Rudhyar, D. *AFA Bulletin,* Washington, D.C., November 20, 1968.

Rudhyar, D. How can astrology's claims be proven valid? *Aquarian Agent,* 1970, 10, 7-9.

Ruperti, A. Astrology and the needs of modern man. *Kosmos,* 1971, 4 (2), 5-8.

Suzuki-roshi, S. *Zen Mind, beginner's mind.* New York: Walker/Weatherhill, 1970.

Teilhard de Chardin, P. Esquisse d'un univers personnel. Paris: May 4, 1936.

Van Dusen, W. The natural depth in man. In C. Rogers & B. Stevens (Eds.), *Person to person: The problem of being human.* Lafayette, Calif.: Real People Press, 1967.

Whyte, L.L. *The next development in man.* New York: H. Holt, 1948.

Whyte, L.L. *Accent on form.* New York: Harper & Bros., 1954.

Chapter 4

Campbell, J. The historical development of mythology. In H.A. Murray (Ed.), *Myth and mythmaking.* New York: George Braziller, 1960.

Carré, M.H. *Phases of thought in medieval England.* Oxford Univer. Press, 1949.

Dobyns, Zipporah. Astrology as a psychological tool. *Aquarian Agent,* 1970, 1 (9), 1.

Jung, C.G. Interview with André Barbault. *Astrologie Moderne,* May 26, 1954.

Jung, C.G. *Archetypes and the collective unconscious.* New York: Bollingen Foundation, 1959.

Jung, C.G. *The structure and dynamics of the psyche.* London: Routledge & Kegan Paul, 1960.

Metzner, R. Astrology: Potential science and intuitive art. *The Journal of Astrological Studies,* 1970, 1, 164-177.

Whitmont, E. Why causality? *Aquarian Agent,* 1970, 1 (13), 8.

Whyte, L.L. *Accent on form.* New York: Harper & Bros., 1954.

Chapter 5

Barnett, L. Quoted in Margaret Hone. *The modern text book of astrology.* London: Fowler, 1951.

Dobyns, Zipporah. The integration of humanistic psychology and astrology. *Kosmos,* 1971, 4 (1), 8-10.

Ebertin, R. *The combination of stellar influences.* Aalen, Germany: Ebertin-Verlag, 1960.

Glynn, T. A link between the alpha state and a scientific basis of astrology. *AFA Bulletin,* 1972, 34 (3), 28-31.

May, R. Existential bases of psychotherapy. *American Journal of Orthopsychiatry,* 1960, 30, 685-695.

Pay, R. Position of planets linked to solar flare prediction. *Technology Week,* May 15, 1967.

Rudhyar, D. *The astrology of personality.* New York: Lucis Publishing, 1936.

Rudhyar, D. *An astrological study of psychological complexes and emotional problems.* Wassenaar, The Netherlands; Servire, 1966.

Rudhyar, D. *The practice of astrology.* Wassenaar, The Netherlands: Servire, 1968.

Rudhyar, D. *Birth patterns for a new humanity.* Wassenaar, The Netherlands: Servire, 1969.

Rudhyar, D. *The planetarization of consciousness.* Wassenaar, The Netherlands: Servire, 1970.

Ruperti, A. Astrology and the needs of modern man. *Kosmos,* 1971, 4 (2), 5-8.

Chapter 6

Bugenthal, J.F.T. *Challenges of humanistic psychology.* New York: McGraw-Hill, 1967.

May, R. Existential bases of psychotherapy. In M. Zax & G. Stricker (Eds.), *The study of abnormal behavior.* (2nd ed.) New York: Macmillan, 1969.

Rogers, C. & Stevens, B. *Person to person: The problem of being human.* Lafayette, Calif.: Real People Press, 1967.

Rudhyar, D. *AFA Bulletin,* November 20, 1968.

Rudhyar, D. *Astrology for new minds.* Lakemont, Ga.: CSA Press, 1969.

Rudhyar, D. Humanistic Astrology. *Aquarian Agent,* 1971, 2 (1), 4-5.

Termerlin, M. On choice and responsibility in a humanistic psychology. *Journal of Humanistic Psychology,* 1963, 3 (1).

CRCS Books

THE ANCIENT SCIENCE OF GEOMANCY:Living in Harmony with the Earth by Nigel Pennick $12.95. The best and most accessible survey of this ancient wholistic art/science, superbly illustrated with 120 photos.

AN ASTROLOGICAL GUIDE TO SELF-AWARENESS by Donna Cunningham, M.S.W. $7.95. Written in a lively style, this book includes chapters on transits, houses, interpreting aspects, etc. A popular book translated into 5 languages.

THE ART OF CHART INTERPRETATION: A Step-by-Step Method of Analyzing,Synthesizing & Understanding the Birth Chart by Tracy Marks $7.95. A guide to determining the most important features of a birth chart. A must for students!

THE ASTROLOGER'S GUIDE TO COUNSELING: Astrology's Role in the Helping Professions by Bernard Rosenblum, M.D. $7.95. Establishes astrological counseling as a valid and legitimate helping profession. A break-through book!

THE ASTROLOGER'S MANUAL: Modern Insights into an Ancient Art by Landis Knight Green $10.95, 240 pages. A strikingly original work that includes extensive sections on relationships, aspects, and all the fundamentals in a lively new way.

THE ASTROLOGICAL HOUSES: The Spectrum of Individual Experience by Dane Rudhyar $8.95. A recognized classic of modern astrology that has sold over 100,000 copies, this book is required reading for every student of astrology seeking to understand the deeper meanings of the houses.

ASTROLOGY: The Classic Guide to Understanding Your Horoscope by Ronald C. Davison $7.95. The most popular book on astrology during the 1960's & 1970's is now back in print in a new edition, with an instructive new foreword that explains how the author's remarkable keyword system can be used by even the novice student of astrology.

ASTROLOGY FOR THE NEW AGE: An Intuitive Approach by Marcus Allen $7.95. Emphasizes self-acceptance and tuning in to your chart with a positive openness. Helps one create his or her own interpretation.

ASTROLOGY IN MODERN LANGUAGE by Richard Vaughan $12.95, 336 pages. An in-depth interpretation of the birth chart focusing on the houses and their ruling planets-- including the Ascendant and its ruler. A unique, strikingly original work.

ASTROLOGY, KARMA & TRANSFORMATION: The Inner Dimensions of the Birth Chart by Stephen Arroyo $10.95. An insightful book on the use of astrology for persoal growth, seen in the light of the theory of karma and the urge toward self-transformation. International best-seller!

THE ASTROLOGY OF SELF-DISCOVERY: An In-Depth Exploration of the Potentials Revealed in Your Birth Chart by Tracy Marks $9.95, 288 pages. Emphasizes the Moon and its nodes, Neptune, Pluto, & the outer planet transits. An important and brilliantly original work!

ASTROLOGY, PSYCHOLOGY AND THE FOUR ELEMENTS: An Energy Approach to Astrology & Its Use in the Counseling Arts by Stephen Arroyo $9.95. An international best-seller, this book deals with the use of astrology as a practical method of understanding one's attunement to universal forces. Clearly shows how to approach astrology with a real understanding of the energies involved. Awarded the British Astrological Assn's Astrology Prize. A classic translated into 8 languages!

CYCLES OF BECOMING: The Planetary Pattern of Growth by Alexander Ruperti $12.95, 274 pages. The first complete treatment of transits from a humanistic and holistic perspective. All important planetary cycles are correlated with the essential phases of personal development. A pioneering work!

DYNAMICS OF ASPECT ANALYSIS: New Perceptions in Astrology by Bil Tierney $8.95, 288 pages. Ground-breaking work! The most in-depth treatment of aspects and aspect patterns available, including both major and minor configurations. Also includes retrogrades, unaspected planets & more!

A JOURNEY THROUGH THE BIRTH CHART: Using Astrology on Your Life Path by Joanne Wickenburg $7.95. Gives the reader the tools to put the pieces of the birth chart together for self-understanding and encourages creative interpretation by helping the reader to think through the endless combinations of astrological symbols.

THE JUPITER/SATURN CONFERENCE LECTURES: New Insights in Modern Astrology by Stephen Arroyo & Liz Greene $8.95. Talks included deal with myth, chart synthesis, relationships, & Jungian psychology related to astrology. A wealth of original & important ideas!

THE LITERARY ZODIAC by Paul Wright $12.95, 240 pages. A pioneering work, based on extensive research, exploring the connection between astrology and literary creativity.

NUMBERS AS SYMBOLS FOR SELF-DISCOVERY: Exploring Character & Destiny with Numerology by Richard Vaughan $8.95, 336 pages. A how-to book on personal analysis and forecasting your future through Numerology. Examples include the number patterns of a thousand famous personalities.

THE OUTER PLANETS & THEIR CYCLES: The Astrology of the Collective by Liz Greene $7.95. Deals with the individual's attunement to the outer planets as well as with significant historical and generational trends that correlate to these planetary cycles.

PLANETARY ASPECTS: FROM CONFLICT TO COOPERATION: How to Make Your Stressful Aspects Work for You by Tracy Marks $8.95, 225 pages. This revised edition of HOW TO HANDLE YOUR T-SQUARE focuses on the creative understanding of the stressful aspects and focuses on the T-Square configuration both in natal charts and as formed by transits & progressions. The most thorough treatment of these subjects in print!

THE PLANETS AND HUMAN BEHAVIOR by Jeff Mayo $7.95. A pioneering exploration of the symbolism of the planets, blending their modern psychological significance with their ancient mythological meanings. Includes many tips on interpretation.

PRACTICAL PALMISTRY: A Positive Approach from a Modern Perspective by David Brandon-Jones $8.95, 268 pages. This easy-to-use book describes and illustrates all the basics of traditional palmistry and then builds upon that with more recent discoveries based upon the author's extensive experience and case studies. A discriminating approach to an ancient science that includes many original ideas!

THE PRACTICE AND PROFESSION OF ASTROLOGY: Rebuilding Our Lost Connections with the Cosmos by Stephen Arroyo $7.95. A challenging, often controversial treatment of astrology's place in modern society and of astrological counseling as both a legitimate profession and a healing process.

REINCARNATION THROUGH THE ZODIAC by Joan Hodgson $6.50. A study of the signs of the zodiac from a spiritual perspective, based upon the development of different phases of conciousness through reincarnation.

RELATIONSHIPS & LIFE CYCLES: Modern Dimensions of Astrology by Stephen Arroyo $8.95. Thorough discussion of natal chart indicators of one's capacity and need for relationship; techniques of chart comparison; using transits practically; and the use of the houses in chart comparison.

SEX & THE ZODIAC: An Astrological Guide to Intimate Relationships by Helen Terrell $7.95, 256 pages. Goes into great detail in describing and analyzing the dominant traits of women and men as indicated by their Zodiacal signs.

THE SPIRAL OF LIFE: Unlocking Your Potential with Astrology by Joanne Wickenburg & Virginia Meyer $7.95. Covering all astrological factors, this book shows how understanding the birth pattern is an exciting path toward increased self-awareness.

A SPIRITUAL APPROACH TO ASTROLOGY: A Complete Textbook of Astrology by Myrna Lofthus $12.95, 444 pages. A complete astrology textbook from a karmic viewpoint, with an especially valuable 130-page section on karmic interpretation of all aspects, including the Ascendant & MC.

HEALTH BUILDING: The Conscious Art of Living Well by Dr. Randolph Stone $8.95. A complete health program for people of all ages, based on vital energy currents. Includes instructions on vegetarian & purifying diets and energizing exercises for vitality & beauty. The author is the originator of Polarity Therapy.

HELPING YOURSELF WITH NATURAL REMEDIES: An Encyclopedic Guide to Herbal & Nutritional Treatment by Terry Willard, Ph.D. $11.95. This easily accessible book blends 20th century scientific & clinical experience with traditional methods of health maintenance. Allows you to select natural remedies for over 100 specific problems, all arranged in alphabetical order & with a complete index.

POLARITY THERAPY:VOL.I & II The Complete Collected Works by Dr. Randolph Stone, D.O., D.C. $25.00 each. The original books on this revolutionary healing art, available for the first time in trade editions. Fully illustrated with charts & diagrams. Sewn binding.

For more complete information on our books, a complete booklist, or to order any of the above publications, WRITE TO:

**CRCS Publications
Post Office Box 1460
Sebastopol, California 95473
U.S.A.**